Gunning for Sea Ducks

Gunning
for Sea Ducks

BY GEORGE HOWARD GILLELAN

Tidewater Publishers
CENTREVILLE, MARYLAND

The maps in Chapter 3 are adapted, by permission, from
Frank C. Bellrose, *Ducks, Geese and Swans of North America,* a
Wildlife Management Institute book, Stackpole Books, publisher.

Library of Congress Cataloging-in-Publication Data

Gillelan, G. Howard.
  Gunning for sea ducks / by George Howard Gillelan.
    p.   cm.
  Includes   index.
  ISBN   0-87033-386-0
  1. Duck shooting. 2. Sea birds. I. Title.
SK333.D8G55 1988
799.2'44—dc19   88-22036
                                                      CIP

Manufactured in the United States of America
First edition

To my parents, in memoriam,
Mary Elizabeth MacDowell Gillelan
and Joshua Thomas Gillelan

Contents

Foreword

THE REQUEST that I do this foreword to George Howard
Gillelan's book about sea ducks surprised me. But it
shouldn't have, for Howard Gillelan introduced me to the
world of sea-duck hunting. More years ago than either of
us likes to think about, Gillelan invited me to hunt Canada
geese on a piece of land he owned on Maryland's Eastern
Shore. Because Canada geese have been a lifelong passion
of mine, I gladly accepted. The hunting was good—much
too good. We had limits before 8:30 in the morning—and a
whole wonderful day loomed ahead of us with nothing we
had to do. Howard suggested sea ducks. I demurred. "Too
easy to hit those stupid birds," said I. With a superior smirk,
Howard said, "Let's see if you can hit them—they're smaller
than geese." We checked in with a waterman friend of his
and loaded the boat half-full of decoys. "Decoys?" No, these
were Clorox jugs painted dull-black and strung together on
long ropes so that we only needed one anchor to secure a
dozen jugs—excuse me, deeks. Those jugs proved that sea
ducks weren't too bright, or so I thought.

Positioned in the wide-open Chesapeake Bay, half a
mile from any land, and within sight of the big ships moving
up to Baltimore, we swung to our own anchor while half a
hundred jugs swung on theirs.

Gunning for Sea Ducks

"You've got the first shot," said Howard, "and here comes a bunch of scoters."

Heavy-bodied, with fast wingbeats—the black birds were coming right at me. Suicide! Steadying my legs against the roll and pitch of the oyster-tonging boat that served as our shooting platform, I drew a careful bead and shot my first scoter! But he didn't fall! He simply raised his flight path about ten feet, so that he passed directly over me. Tracking his hurtling form, I touched off the second charge, just as the boat lurched to the movement of a wave. I knew that shot went five feet over the flock of scoters. But they were still in range, going away—easiest shot of all. I swung on the tail-end bird and touched it off again, and saw my first scoter collapse among the far string of decoys.

I had learned one lesson—scoters are not as easy to hit as they seem to be, especially when the shooting platform is rolling in the waves.

Sea ducks seemed unafraid of us that day—and for my part, they were right. Common scoters and oldsquaws came over us, past us, around us—not changing their flight pattern in any way after they saw us. After almost every flight, we'd slip our anchor and use the boat to pick up the dead birds. As we worked, Howard talked about sea ducks, about the wild, cold, distant lands where they produced their young, about their diet, about their migration paths, about the fact that many of these sea ducks never saw a human being until they had migrated 500 miles south of their nesting places.

Obviously, George Howard Gillelan was interested in sea ducks. He aroused the same interest in me. And for that, I thank him!

Charles L. "Chuck" Cadieux

Albuquerque, New Mexico

Gunning for Sea Ducks

CHAPTER 1

Sea Ducks: An Introduction

JUST EXACTLY WHAT are sea ducks? If you don't know, you have plenty of company—about 220 million Americans, including the majority of those seasoned waterfowl hunters who hunt the better-known species.

Sea ducks are about as similar to well-known duck species as a wild tom turkey is to a tufted titmouse. The only thing the latter have in common is that they're both birds, and the only thing a mallard has in common with a sea duck is that they're both birds with webbed feet.

Before writing another line about sea ducks, it's in order to clarify what they are. The term "sea ducks" is a misnomer. It's true that these birds are found in the oceans off both coasts of North America, but during the winter they're at home in inland waters such as the Great Lakes and the Chesapeake Bay. While they're pursued by some waterfowlers in the Atlantic and the Pacific, it seems apparent that most sea-duck hunting takes place in waters far away from the sea.

A good example of the misnaming of the sea-duck group is the situation in Maryland, where I've had most of my experience with sea-duck shooting. Maryland's eastern border is the Atlantic Ocean, but most of the hunting for these birds takes place not in the open sea but in the waters of the Chesapeake Bay. There is a limited amount of sea-duck shooting in the Atlantic offshore of the Ocean City region and south of there off the Virginia coast, but it's of marginal interest to most coastal gunners, who prefer to go slightly inland on the bays west of the barrier islands, where they shoot the usual duck species.

Generally, the birds that are categorized as sea ducks in the mid-Atlantic area are the three different kinds of scoters (surf scoters, whitewings, and common, or American, scoters) and oldsquaws. In more northerly regions, such as New England and Alaska, there are harlequin ducks and several types of eiders, the latter being popular among gunners off the Maine coast. However, harlequins and eiders seldom winter as far south as the Chesapeake. Some waterfowl biologists include buffleheads, goldeneyes, and mergansers in the sea-duck category, but for our purposes the term "sea ducks" means the previously mentioned species.

Because sea ducks are at present largely ignored by gunners in the Chesapeake and a lot of other bodies of water where they're prevalent, they can be thought of as the sleeping beauties of the waterfowl world. They're not considered in the same breath as the glamour ducks, beginning with the currently non-shootable canvasbacks. Cans were the supreme species of yesteryear, because of their vast wintering numbers on the Susquehanna Flats and their delectability as prime table fare.

Except for a couple of limited sessions, the hunting season on canvasbacks has been discontinued in Maryland since 1972, yet still their numbers are in decline, proving that gunning pressure is a secondary reason for the tragic plummeting of canvasback populations, as well as the decline of other duck populations. Pintails, black ducks, and other species have decreased in numbers critically, due to the destruction of the wetlands where they habitually

4

The author with his favorite sea duck, a drake oldsquaw.
Photograph courtesy of Chuck Cadieux.

nested during the spring and summer. Those nesting grounds are mostly in the north-central United States and the prairie provinces of Canada.

Sea ducks, on the other hand, have escaped the drying up and destruction of their nesting grounds, because they breed and raise their young much farther north, in Alaska and the Arctic and sub-Arctic tundra regions of Canada.

It is for this reason that their populations are fairly stable, the birds are abundant, and the hunting seasons and bag limits for them are the most liberal of those for all ducks. If these trends among all ducks continue, it seems likely that sea ducks will represent the best waterfowl hunting of tomorrow.

A more comprehensive explanation of the ornithology of the different sea ducks will be found in Chapter 3; but for now, let's approach sea ducks from the sportsman's perspective.

CHAPTER 2

Let's Go Sea-Ducking

INSTEAD OF RAMBLING on about the taxonomy of this unique type of waterfowl, important though that is, we're going to start off with a bang—or, more precisely, with several hundred bangs before the end of this chapter. The reader will join a party of gunners on a sea-duck shoot, in this case with a commercial guide.

Actually, our shoot begins weeks before a trigger is pulled on a sea duck. We're on the Eastern Shore of Maryland, where the Chesapeake Bay, its tributaries, and adjacent farms are internationally famous for goose hunting. Upward of a half-million Canada geese, together with growing gaggles of snow geese, are fall and winter guests in this region. Also in the category of big birds that are winter visitors to the Eastern Shore are increasing thousands of tundra swans, known until a few years ago as whistling swans. There's no hunting season for the large, pure-white invaders at this time; but because of the growth in their numbers and their depredation of winter-wheat crops, it seems fairly likely that they'll be legally hunted before the end of this decade.

Sea ducks are considered the poor relations of the duck family by the majority of Maryland's gunners, who are more interested in mallards, black ducks, pintails, and other popular species. However, for those ducks, gunners are subjected to an abbreviated season, reduced bag limits, and drastically fewer birds compared to the halcyon years when flocks of canvasbacks and black ducks literally darkened the sky.

There are two reasons for the general lack of interest in sea-duck hunting. One is that the majority of water-fowlers have little or no knowledge of sea ducks, nor are they aware of the fact that an assault on these birds offers fast, sporty shooting. The other reason is that sea ducks are thought to be inedible, and the genuine sportsman refrains from shooting game that can't be utilized on the dinner table. This book will educate both groups of people—those whose knowledge of sea ducks is either lacking or sparse, and those who mistakenly believe that sea ducks are unfit for human consumption.

The initial preparatory step in our sortie after sea ducks is to note the long-awaited announcement of the hunting season on the birds. The U.S. Fish and Wildlife Service, after aerial surveys that indicate conditions on the far-north nesting grounds, computerizes its estimates of the populations of various kinds of waterfowl, and sets the parameters of the season's dates and bag limits. Within that framework, the individual states determine the length and bag limits of their seasons.

In this partially fictionalized version of an actual 1986 outing for sea ducks, the regulations are fairly typical of those of previous years. The 107-day season (excluding Sundays, on which there is no hunting of any kind in Maryland) is from October 6 to January 20, 1987, with a daily bag limit of seven birds and a possession limit of 14. Compare that to the four-bird limit for other ducks, the season on which is November 18 to January 3. That's only 47 days, again excluding Sundays. There are certain exceptions to those latter dates, among them a special two-day duck season—October 10 and 11—to allow hunting for early arrivals passing through on their way south, and a brief respite for all waterfowl during the state's firearms deer season—November 29 to December 6.

In the Maryland portion of the Chesapeake Bay, sea ducks may be hunted only in a designated zone, a regulation that is of little practical concern, because the major concentrations of the birds are located within that zone.

So now, we know when the season starts on sea ducks—early October in this case. It's a month before the opening day, and we're busy with the mourning-dove season, which started on September 1. Shooting at doves is a challenge for scattergunners. The national average is one dove for every five shots fired. These birds are difficult targets, not because of their speed in flight, but because of their erratic, unpredictable flight patterns. Most dove shooters endear themselves to ammo manufacturers, because of the high number of shots the average gunner takes on a good dove shoot; however, the above-average marksman, given a productive field for dove shooting, can down his limit of 12 doves with less than a full box of 25 shells in a few hours.

Dove shooting is not particularly good practice for sea-duck hunting for several reasons. The zig-zag, up-and-down flight of a dove is nothing like the much-speedier, straight-line flight of a skein of sea ducks. Doves, not being encased in a thick skin beneath an armorlike covering of heavy feathers, are easier to bring down. Also, in dove shooting we use light loads, smaller shot, and guns with a fairly open bore. Then too, the temperature during the early dove season calls for shirt-sleeves as opposed to the foul-weather clothing that's required for much of the sea-duck season. Nevertheless, a dove shoot gives us a chance to burn some powder, to sharpen our shooting eyes, and to practice properly mounting the shotgun in a hurry.

Gunning for Sea Ducks

Before we raise the curtain on a *sui generis* brand of waterfowling, we must do some backstage work, organizing our cast and getting our props lined up.

Early on, I had engaged our guide, Norman Haddaway, who, along with Leonard Falcone, operates an outfit that takes out fishing parties during the summer and seaduckers during the hunting season. Among a number of competing guides, none of whom I'd ever gunned with, I had selected Haddaway for two reasons. First, I had been impressed when I fished with the Haddaway-Falcone combination three months earlier in a benefit fishing tournament sponsored by Ducks Unlimited. Their expert seamanship and boat-handling were as impressive as were their enthusiasm and their concern for their clients. The result was that our boat was one of the winners in the tournament. The other reason I booked a sea-duck hunt with Norm Haddaway was that he didn't criticize his competitors.

A few weeks after the start of the sea-duck season, I called Haddaway for a report. He said the shooting had been fairly good, but that the major numbers of sea ducks had not yet arrived. That's why I'd booked my hunt for early November. I figured that by then most if not all of the sea ducks wintering on the Chesapeake would have settled in. Also, I reasoned that after a month of sea-ducking, Haddaway and Falcone would have located the birds and shaken down their guiding procedure.

In the ensuing weeks, I called Haddaway several more times, to ascertain the success of his hunting parties. His reports were reassuring. Thousands of scoters and oldsquaws had been sighted. Most of his clients had taken their limits, sometimes soon enough to return to the dock at noon or slightly after. Those who failed to limit out, Norm said, either ran out of shells or else were lousy shots.

10

Let's Go Sea-Ducking

Meanwhile, I was busy lining up the other members of my hunting party, being particular about their reliability, their safe gun-handling habits, and their amiability. When you're confined for several hours in the comparatively close quarters of a duck blind, a goose pit, or a sea-ducking boat, any undesirable qualities in your hunting buddies can spoil the outing. I've always been fortunate in not having hunted with poor sportsmen, game hogs, sloppy gunners, or disagreeable companions. This is probably due to the fact that I'm somewhat paranoid about being the guy who organizes a hunt. Even if it's a flop due to an unsatisfactory guide or poor shooting, and you feel responsible, if your gunning companions are selected with care, they'll understand that a lousy day once in a while is part of the game.

The first person I invited on this particular shoot was my son, Ian, who enjoys sea-ducking but hadn't done it for several seasons. I rejected a few other possibilities because of their inexperience or because I'd never gunned with them before. I invited Keith Walters, a writer friend who is the Atlantic Flyway editor of *Waterfowler's World*, and the third member of our group, Eric Mills, then a newspaper reporter for the Easton *Star-Democrat*. (Easton, Maryland, besides being a center for mid-Atlantic waterfowling, is the headquarters of the famous Waterfowl Festival, which annually attracts more than 20,000 people to a town with a population of about 8,000.) As the nongunning member of our hunting party, Eric concentrated on absorbing as much information as possible on the sport of sea-ducking, doing his shooting with a camera, and taking notes furiously. His efforts paid off: He won an award for his illustrated account of our hunt.

To continue the theatrical metaphor mentioned earlier, I had assembled the cast, now it was time to get the props in order.

11

Gunning for Sea Ducks

First, the gun. I took my old Marlin 12-gauge over-and-under, bored modified and full choke. Admittedly, it's not the ideal shotgun for waterfowling, but I shoot fairly well with it, because I use it on everything—doves, pheasants, quail, geese, rabbits, and squirrels. As fodder to feed the scattergun, I had four boxes of No. 4 high-brass shells. I checked the shotgun to make sure it was not loaded, put it back into its padded case, and placed it the night before on a pile with the shell bag beside the front door. Also on the pile were my down-lined hunting jacket, cap, and gloves.

Before bedding down, I constructed a pair of hefty sandwiches and set out my Thermos bottle for a filling of hot coffee the next morning. I laid out my rubber-bottom boots and several layers of clothing—a T-shirt, a warm turtleneck, and a heavy wool Scottish fisherman's sweater.

I checked my camera and film, and made sure my hunting license, plus federal and state waterfowl stamps, was in the pocket of my hunting jacket. As a final thought, due to the weather forecast, I added to my kit a supply of Kleenex, for wiping the predicted rain from my eyeglasses.

By prior arrangement I was to pick up Eric Mills in Easton at 6 A.M., and rendezvous with the others at the marina in Tilghman where the guide kept his boat. Arriving at the appointed time, I was relieved to see a light in the window of Eric's third-floor apartment. At least he was up and dressing; this was his first hunting experience and I hadn't been sure that he'd be ready on time.

The town still slumbered. In my rearview mirror I saw the approach of a state-police patrol car, clearly recognizable under the street lights. I was double-parked, with my headlights on. The trooper slowed his car and gave me a once-over when he was abreast of me. I waved to him in vague salutation, although I didn't know him. Apparently satisfied that I was up to no illegal deviltry, he drove on.

Let's Go Sea-Ducking

The street was dead-still. I was wide awake, bright-eyed with anticipation. I thought of George Will's description: ". . . the sharp sensations of morning—freshness and sobriety and a second chance." Raindrops, only a few, spotted my windshield. Eric's light went out. He appeared a moment later and we were off.

"I hope you brought rain gear," I said.

"I sure did," he replied. "Also, I brought just about all the heavy clothes I own."

Because it was his first experience at this sort of thing and this was a story assignment for his paper, I utilized the 40-minute drive to our Tilghman departure point by giving him some background about sea-ducking and hunting in general.

Waxing philosophical, I cited the opinion of the late Spanish philosopher, José Ortega y Gasset (1883-1955), who had meditated that hunting is the natural order of things. In hunting, according to Ortega, man becomes part of nature. He added, "One does not hunt in order to kill; on the contrary, one kills in order to have hunted."

"If I interpret it correctly, I wholly agree with that," I told Eric. "I believe that the kill is secondary. To me, what's important is the hunt itself and the anticipation and the companionship and the test of one's marksmanship, and, to use a cliché, 'the thrill of the chase.' I can enjoy myself without firing a shot, just being outdoors. It's definitely not a macho thing, as some people believe, although I suppose to some hunters, the macho angle is the big thing."

Having unburdened myself of some of my personal philosophy, I reminisced for Eric's benefit and my own nostalgia about some of my experiences in 20 years of sea-duck hunting.

On my first sea-duck hunt, we didn't start until 10:30 A.M.—which gave my hunting buddy and me time to bag

13

three ducks apiece from a blind in front of the house I then had on the water. They weren't sea ducks, of course; as I recall, they were all buffleheads.

That late departure time is a point of disagreement between most commercial hunting guides and me. In my experience, admittedly parochial, it matters not at all what time you start on a sea-duck hunt. I've found that if the birds are in the waters to be hunted, you'll get shooting pretty much throughout the day.

But almost all guides insist on starting around daybreak. That means you must roll out of bed at an hour that's totally uncivilized, even for an early riser like me, because you'll probably have to drive some distance to the guide's take-off point.

As to the reason for their insistence in this regard, I really don't know. Perhaps they honestly believe it's necessary to start at an unrealistically early hour. To be cynical about it, it could be perversity on their part, or the tough pro's sadistic satisfaction in inconveniencing a soft-living dude sportsman. Sometimes I suspect it's because they're anxious for clients to get their limits as soon as possible, so they can get the boat cleaned up and attend to other matters before the day is over. That's a reasonable explanation and, if that's their motivation, I can't blame them too much.

Occasionally I think I'll be forceful and say, "Look, it's my money I'm spending, and I'll be the one to decide on our starting time." But if I do that, I can imagine what will happen: The shooting will be either slow or nonexistent, and the guide will say, "Don't blame me. If we'd gotten out there early like I wanted, we'd have had a terrific shoot." So I'll go along, however reluctantly, with starting a sea-duck hunt at an ungodly hour.

Coming back to that first venture for sea ducks, my friend Earl Shelsby and I were the guests of a nonprofessional guide, who had some experience in the then comparatively new sport of sea-duck hunting. He was Francis Howard, a crack shot and owner of a successful sporting goods store catering to local Eastern Shore sportsmen as well as hundreds of visiting gunners and anglers.

It was a sunny, bright, fairly calm, early fall day, and two of our lady friends had decked out—literally—a super alfresco spread for our luncheon. I mention the weather in particular, because it was not an ideal day for shooting the traditional duck species (more on that subject later).

Francis chugged his 35-foot craft—a typical Eastern Shore workboat—out of the harbor of Tilghman, a quaint watermen's village bordering the Chesapeake Bay, for the 30-minute run out to the sea-duck zone. Before we cleared the harbor we passed several dozen oldsquaws swimming placidly among the moored boats. That was my introduction to sea-ducking: You can't shoot these birds outside the legally designated sea-duck zone, and you must find large concentrations of sea ducks before setting out the anchor and beginning serious shooting.

Francis binoculared the waters ahead. After spotting a raft of a hundred or so sitting sea ducks a quarter of a mile away, he cut the motor, threw over the anchor, and began dispersing his spread of decoys.

These were full-bodied fake birds, which he had cooked up in his kitchen oven from expandable polystyrene. As I recall, they were scaup (bluebills) and were definitely not ersatz sea ducks. Many a duck hunter has drawn a blank because his decoys looked unnatural or were not strategically placed. But sea ducks apparently have not gotten the message; often they'll decoy to almost anything vaguely resembling one of their breed—for example, plastic bleach bottles or gallon milk jugs painted flat-black with touches of white or gray.

I was soon to witness another common aberration in sea-duck behavior. Here we were, in a snow-white work-

15

boat in brilliant sunlight, wearing no camouflage clothing, moving about freely on deck, jabbering and laughing. Yet, before Francis finished stringing out his lures, a trio of inquisitive scoters zipped by the port side. In mid-sandwich, we fumbled about for our shotguns, which were still in their cases. We quickly forgot about lunch, unsheathed our artillery, and were ready for the next squadron of birds, which accommodated us by passing over the decoys 20 yards away and then probably laughed as our first volley left them unscathed.

When the next group came by to examine our decoy layout, Earl dropped one of the scoters, while the rest of us blasted holes in the autumn air. Francis marked the bird on the water, noted that the slack tide and wind weren't appreciably moving the dead whitewing, and warned us to be ready for action at any moment. In less than three minutes, another flight of the curious, gregarious birds flew by to investigate. As the parade of ducks continued, I blew at least ten more shots before connecting, and the others had about the same average.

As we adjusted somewhat to the range and timing of sea-duck shooting, we improved to some extent. About every other time a duck was hit but only wounded, Francis up-anchored and tracked down the cripple. Then I learned another lesson—sea ducks, even when sitting still on the water, are difficult to subdue. As the following chapter will explain, their diving capability is extraordinary, as are their tolerance for the depths of Davy Jones's locker, and their resistance to shotgun pellets. In a typical cripple recovery, two or three shots (or more) are taken at the sitting duck. He dives. Nobody knows where he'll come up, if at all. Finally, he surfaces 50 yards from the spot where he submerged. The boat heads for him and again three shotguns unleash their charges. Maybe they get him this time, maybe not. The process is repeated until the duck is accounted for.

Oldsquaw drakes have long tail feathers.

Gunning for Sea Ducks

The misses at decoying birds, combined with the amount of ammo expended on running down cripples, is the reason why sea-duckers must each have an arsenal of at least four boxes of shells.

Remembering that the raison d'être for this outing was my assignment to produce a feature story for *Outdoor Life*, a magazine with which I was associated at that time, I broke out my photography gear. Substituting a camera for my shotgun, I lucked into what has to be the best action photo I've ever taken. I was standing directly behind Francis Howard when an oldsquaw drake darted by our decoys. The picture shows the gunner, his semiautomatic shotgun, and the ejected shell hurtling through the air. That's photographic drama enough, but the best is yet to come. The photo also shows the speeding sea duck and the shot pattern hitting the water a good two feet behind the bird. And Francis was one of the best shotgun artists in the area. My respect for the challenge of sea-duck shooting was tripled.

We quit in midafternoon. The balance sheet showed more than three boxes of shells per gunner versus slightly less than our 21-bird limit. It included oldsquaws and all three varieties of scoters.

I learned plenty about sea ducks during my baptism of fire. First, that the sport is addictive: I could hardly wait to set up my next shoot for the toughest-to-kill, fastest-flying birds I've ever hunted. (I agree with someone who likened it to shooting at doves while standing on a rocking chair, particularly in rough seas.) I learned, too, that sea-duck shooting is instructive, because many shots are at low-flying birds, so that you can see your shot pattern hitting the water—often, too often, well behind the target. And when your shooting is on the beam, you know you are leading correctly, because you can see the bird centered in the pattern as the pellets strike the water. But sometimes the big, tough birds, even when centered in a load of No. 4's, don't falter in flight. And not all the sea ducks fly accommodatingly low; when they're silhouetted against the sky, you're not sure why you missed, although nine out of ten times you can figure you shot low or behind them.

Just about the time I'd finished recounting to Eric my first attempt at sea ducks, we arrived at Tilghman for our rendezvous with the guides, who had just pulled into the parking area. In a few minutes, Ian and Keith rolled in. Leonard and Norm helped us stow our gear aboard—shotguns, shell bags, cameras, lunches, extra clothes. Dawn was breaking late because of the clouds and the wind-driven rain.

In less than a half-hour out of port, we were in the open Chesapeake Bay, and the guides teamed up to lay out our decoy spread. They spurned the crude plastic jug decoys in favor of full-bodied replicas of scoters and old-squaws—more than a hundred of them tied down with weighty anchors so they'd hold in the rising breeze and the incoming tide.

The decoys were not completely deployed before a six-pack of scoters, true to form, zoomed past our boat. They were well within range, but we hadn't even loaded our guns. We were prepared weapon-wise when the next bunch charged us—our loaded guns were ready, but the people shooting the guns were not ready. All hands, including the guides, scattered a few hundred lead pellets into the Chesapeake.

A few minutes later, Keith Walters broke the ice by dropping a scoter out of a group of five that were strung out five yards apart in a perfectly straight line formation, about 20 feet over the water. Three of the gunners let fly at the ducks, but it was clearly Keith's shot that accounted for our first sea duck of the day.

We all slapped him on the back and congratulated him for being the first one to score. Though he accepted the praise at the time, being a gentlemen and a true sportsman, he told me a few weeks later that he had been aiming at the leader of the flock and was surprised to see the next one in line crumple and plummet into the water.

There are a couple of lessons in that. First, it shows how fast sea ducks can fly, particularly when they're hustled along by a 20-knot tail wind. Second, it's a good example of the fact that it's smart to aim at the leader of a string of sea ducks; if you don't lead him enough when aiming and you're shooting in a crosswind, there's a fair chance you'll hit the next bird in the line.

On recollection, it seems that there was no more than a five-minute lull between shooting sprees. Everybody got plenty of shooting at the inquisitive, gregarious ducks as they zoomed in to look over the spread of decoys. None were more than 30 feet above the waves, and many skimmed low, only a few feet above the surface. The guides, spotting the birds from a distance, regularly announced which direction the targets were coming from and how many were in an approaching group. Sometimes, Haddaway hollered, "Don't shoot; they're too far away."

A number of flights of big, black birds flew by within range, sometimes in a gooselike formation. If someone in the party raised his gun, Falcone or Haddaway shouted, "Don't shoot. They're cormorants and they're not legal." We also saw a dozen or more big flights of scaup, or blackheads or bluebills, call them what you may. These were groups of 50 to more than 100, and were much too high to shoot at, but just seeing them in such big, black clouds was a kick.

I was shooting from a comfortable seat on the port side, while the others were scattered at various standing or sitting positions across the deck. During one period, most of the ducks crossed our starboard side, and for safety's sake I refrained from shooting because of the others.

Let's Go Sea-Ducking

"I know why all the action is on your side of the boat," I said. "It's because these ducks are smart enough to know I'm on this side, and they won't have a chance if they swing by me."

I was only kidding, of course. I'd bagged a few ducks, but I'd missed plenty of shots and was already into my second box of shells. It was just about then that a single oldsquaw drake appeared from out of nowhere, whipping in from my left. I put a lengthy lead on him, followed through, and pulled the trigger. That was it. Stone dead, instantly. No need to chase down a cripple this time. Such was his speed that before coming to rest on the water, his carcass made two hops across the waves, like a flat stone skipping across the surface of a pond.

"Nice shot," someone said.

"Beautiful shot. That's the way to hit 'em. Not even a wing-flutter," Norm Haddaway said, relieved that he wouldn't have to up-anchor and run down a wounded bird.

A short time afterward, an excited Haddaway yelled over the wind, "My God, here comes a real Jesus Christ bunch from off our stern."

"What's a 'Jesus Christ bunch'?" Eric asked.

"There are so many of them that you don't believe it. You see 'em and say 'Jesus Christ, what a bunch of ducks.' "

That group of about 20 ducks must have been blessed by the Savior, because five shotguns disgorged a pound or so of lead, and the ducks flew on.

"All that shooting and we didn't cut neither feather," Haddaway said, disgusted with his own shooting as much as everyone else's.

And so it continued for the rest of the morning and into the early afternoon. There was never more than a free ten minutes in the action. In the aggregate, several hundred ducks—oldsquaws and all three varieties of scoters—kept us on the alert almost constantly. Some of them approached

21

and veered off at the last minute, but plenty of them provided shooting.

Although we were shy of our limit of 35 ducks, at about 2:30 we told the guides to call it a day. On the way back to port, I remarked to Walters, "With all that great shooting we had out there in the prime sea-duck area of the Chesapeake, we were the only boat. That's a perfect example of the fact that this sport is under-utilized."

While I was driving Eric back to his place in Easton, he asked me to elaborate on my sea-duck hunting experiences. He wanted background for the feature story he was writing, but beyond that he was intrigued with this sport and anxious to learn more about it.

I told him about my 1970 sea-duck shoot with Larry Scharch, a waterman out of Tilghman. Larry was new to the sport, as was most everyone at that time. He had recently returned from Vietnam, where, contrary to the usual Pentagon practice of trying to convert welders into cooks, he had served on a gunboat on the Mekong River.

Larry was 24 at the time, a typical young waterman: Tonging for oysters in the winter and catching crabs during the summer, he was following the occupational lifestyle of generations of Eastern Shoremen. His hunting boat was the same rugged craft he used for crabbing and oystering. As a special concession to his hunting clients, he had a stove installed in the small forward cabin of his workboat.

To digress for a moment, there's one thing that tends to lower the individual satisfaction level when several gunners and a guide are in a boat or a blind or a goose pit. A quartet of ducks or geese buzz your decoys. All hands blaze away, and a couple of birds hit the drink or thud down in a cut-over cornfield. Usually, there's no way of determining for sure whose shooting it was that brought down one or more of the birds.

Left to right, Guides Norm Haddaway and Leonard Falcone with author's son, Ian, and some of the sea ducks taken on the hunt described in the text.

Gunning for Sea Ducks

Sometimes you can tell if you missed or if one of the birds seemed to roll off your gun barrel. But you can't be absolutely positive, because of the fine art of "claiming." If you believe you dropped one of the birds, you'd better put in your claim immediately. If you don't, the guide or another hunter will say something like, "Gee, I really nailed that one." Maybe he did, maybe not. Maybe he honestly thought he downed the fowl, or maybe he knew damned well he missed; but he figured there was nothing to lose by staking his claim. When a group shoots, who can prove absolutely whose gun dropped the quarry? The end result is that you're robbed of the satisfaction of knowing for sure that your shooting was on the beam.

That was the main reason I engaged Larry Scharch on a party-of-one shoot. The other reason was that I was anxious to go sea-ducking soon again and didn't have time to enlist some other gunners. That shoot was very rewarding. I blew plenty of shots and wasted my share of ammo, but I learned a lot about estimating the ducks' speed and how much to lead them. And when a duck hit the water, I knew for sure that I was responsible, because Larry wasn't shooting. It was a satisfying outing, and—as icing on the cake—when I was loading my car, Larry gave me a half-bushel of fresh oysters that his father had tonged that morning.

As soon as I got a chance, I booked Larry Scharch for another sea-duck sortie. This time, I undertook to enlarge the education of my then-teenage son, Ian, by taking him out of school for a day of sea-ducking. He was 15 at the time, and he could handle his 20-gauge Beretta Silver Snipe over-and-under well enough to break 15 out of 25 clay birds thrown from a hand trap. The education he got that day was quite a bit different from wrestling with trig problems and trying to make sense out of Chaucerian English.

Let's Go Sea-Ducking

It didn't take long—about ten shots within five minutes—for Ian to appreciate the difference between powdering a slow-moving clay bird and contending with the jet-propelled speed of a sea duck. After about 35 rounds, he got the knack and collected a few birds. Meanwhile, I was using my newly acquired sea-ducking expertise, by splashing about three ducks for each box of shells, including the shots taken while running down the elusive cripples.

As usual, Larry didn't bring his shotgun. When the birds' activity slowed for a few minutes, he asked if he could try my gun on the next batch of ducks that came in. I said, "Sure. Larry, show us how it's done."

With that, a pair of oldsquaws paid us a visit to look over Larry's plastic-jug decoys. Using a shotgun he had never before handled, he knocked down one bird, swung smoothly on the other and got it, too. A neat double, with an unfamiliar gun, yet.

"Just luck," he said.

"Look out, Larry. Here come three more. Let's see you do a repeat," I said. He emptied both barrels and got nothing but breezy salt air. I often wonder if he missed deliberately, so as not to make us look bad.

"I told you it was just luck," he said, handing the gun back to me. My confidence was restored a few minutes later, when two whitewing scoters passed us astern: Ian and I teamed up and took both ducks.

The birds were so plentiful and flying so steadily that day, that I figured I'd try a couple of experiments on sea ducks—using a standard duck call, and trying to wave them in with some moving object. Possibly others had tried those tricks before on sea ducks, but I'd never heard of anyone crazy enough to do it.

I asked Larry if he'd ever heard of anyone who had tried waving in or calling sea ducks. He said he hadn't. He added what most waterfowlers know: that there are times when waving a cap or handkerchief may attract flights of ducks or Canada geese. But he'd never heard of anyone trying it on sea ducks. As for using a duck call, he said it might work, because some sea ducks are known to utter a faint one- or two-note call. Anyway, both attempts were fairly successful, and will be covered more thoroughly in Chapter 5.

Over the next couple of years, I introduced a number of other gunning friends to sea-ducking with Larry Scharch. Some were bigwigs with the Interior Department's Fish and Wildlife Service. All were experienced waterfowlers who were new to this sport. Without exception, they were completely flabbergasted by the speed of sea ducks, their unorthodox behavior, and how difficult they are to hit.

Incidentally, when my sea-duck story finally appeared in the July 1972 issue of *Outdoor Life,* the headline—which I did not write—was "Fastest Shooting in the East." That's dead wrong; it's incorrect by the length of the United States, because I maintain that the frenzied pace of a good sea-duck shoot represents the fastest shooting from the Eastern Seaboard to the West Coast, plus a few places in between.

Now that we've developed a sore right shoulder from shooting so many sea ducks, let's learn more about these birds from the scientific angle.

CHAPTER 3

Sea Ducks:
Their Habits and Habitat

As STATED PREVIOUSLY, when we refer to sea ducks, we're considering scoters, eiders, oldsquaws, and harlequin ducks. If we were living 150 years ago, we would have included Labrador ducks.

The reason for the extinction of the Labrador duck *(Camptorhynchus labradorius)* is not clear. The last one of the species was shot near Long Island, New York, in 1875. Although John J. Audubon, the great naturalist-artist, never sighted a live specimen of a Labrador duck, there is, fortunately, a mounted group of the birds in the American Museum of Natural History, in New York City.

The species got its name from its principal breeding area, the coast of Labrador, though it was plentiful in the Gulf of St. Lawrence and probably bred there, too. During the winter, Labrador ducks favored the New England coast, but were unknown south of Long Island. Not very tasty, the birds were not sought after as food, especially in view of the fact that there was an abundance of more desirable table ducks at that time. It has been speculated that the extermination of the Labrador duck was due to feather hunters and the predators, both human and animal, who raided the nests and collected eggs for food.

Gunning for Sea Ducks

It would be a gross mistake to conclude that sea ducks follow a standard pattern in their behavior. Although oldsquaws, scoters, eiders, and harlequin ducks are considered sea ducks, the habits of these species reflect an individuality that can be likened to the social melting pot of the polyglot United States in the last century. In other words, there are sea ducks and there are sea ducks, just as there are Americans and there are Americans. A scoter is in many ways as different from an oldsquaw as a Dixieland jazz musician is from a Viking-blooded farmer in Minnesota, or a Downeast Maine potato grower is from a Texas rancher.

Although the decoying behavior of most sea ducks during the hunting season is not vastly different, their wintering and spring-summer nesting grounds are not at all patternized. About the only thing the sea-duck species have in common is that they nest in the far north, well away from the agricultural areas where most other ducks are threatened by drainage of their pothole breeding grounds. And that is what is largely responsible for the stability of sea-duck populations.

Oldsquaws (*Clangula hyemalis*) are known, more logically, in Britain as "long-tailed ducks," because of the lengthy tail feathers of the male, whose coloration is more interesting than that of the drab female, a characteristic which prevails notably amongst mallards, teal, baldpates, pintails, wood ducks, canvasbacks, and some other species.

One reason I have a particular fondness for oldsquaws, apart from the graceful, jaunty tail feathers and the pretty plumage of the male, is that the first sea duck I ever shot was an oldsquaw. That was in 1947, long before anyone thought about having a season on sea ducks in my part of the country. It was in the remote waters off Tangier, an isolated island community in the Virginia section of the Chesa-

28

A decorative decoy carving of a drake oldsquaw

peake Bay. At that time, Tangier Islanders, their speech not having been polluted by radio and television, spoke a dialect similar to Elizabethan English, which was only half-intelligible to a mainland city slicker from Baltimore, which was where I lived then.

When I downed the duck and the guide retrieved it, I was unable to identify the bird. The guide said it was a "Suddley Duck." "Sure," I said. "That's exactly what I thought it is, a 'Suddley Duck.' " Actually, I'd never heard the term, and had no idea what kind of duck I'd bagged.

As soon as I returned from that shooting trip, I pored over several waterfowl books and finally found what I was looking for. Although on the Tangier hunt, I had been after other prey—canvasbacks, redheads, and black ducks—I learned that I had shot an oldsquaw.

The species has more colloquial monikers than any other duck I know of. Among them are: Swallow-tailed Duck, Old Wife, Old Injun, Old Molly, Old Billy, John Connolly, Uncle Huldy, Coween or Cowheen, Calloo, Cockawee, Scoldenore, Scolder, Quandy, Squeaking Duck, Callithumpian Duck, Granny, Ha-ha-way, Hell's Chicken, Jack-owly, Mommy, Knockmolly, Jay-eye-see, Mammy Duck, Organ Duck, Siwash, Winter Duck, Hound, and South-southerly.

The only rationale for some of those regional names for oldsquaws is the fact that they're forever chattering among themselves, especially in the spring. The name that stuck, "oldsquaw," was apparently handed down by some Cree Indians, who were reminded by the birds of the constant jabbering of their wives. In the opinion of some observers, no wildfowl, aside from Canada geese, are so noisy when resting on the water.

What helped me identify the bird I'd brought home as an oldsquaw was a picture of the species in one of the bird books. The same book listed the colloquial names. When I

Sea Ducks: Their Habits and Habitat

saw "South-southerly" among the names, it rang a bell that "Suddley Duck" was the Tangier Island guide's abbreviated version of "South-southerly."

The call of the oldsquaw, which is responsible for its many nicknames, can be heard for a mile or more on a windless day, or if the birds are rafted upwind. To some peoples' ears, the oldsquaws' garrulous conversations sound like a pack of hounds baying in the distance, while others are reminded of the sound of an organ. The call sounds like "ow-ow-owdle-ow," or "caloo-caloo-caloo," or "ahahlowet," depending on the imaginative description of the listener.

Typically a drake oldsquaw is about 20 inches long and weighs 2 pounds; the smaller female is a bit over 15 inches in length and weighs less than 2 pounds. Because their bodies are more streamlined than those of scoters and eiders, oldsquaws are capable of flying more than 70 miles per hour, although their average flight speed is about 50 miles per hour.

There are an estimated three to four million oldsquaws scattered around North America, plus undetermined numbers in Siberia, Greenland, Iceland, and possibly other remote Arctic areas. If the *Guinness Book of Records* included waterfowl, oldsquaws would be listed in two categories: 1) they nest in greater numbers in the northernmost part of the world than any other duck, and 2) they dive deeper, using both wings and feet, for food than any other duck, having been found dead in the nets of commercial fishermen set at over 200 feet.

The oldsquaw's nesting area extends to within 500 miles of the North Pole. They prefer to hatch and raise their young in barren-ground tundra or in Arctic coastal areas encircling the subpolar regions. They breed also in Alaska, the Bering Sea, Baffin Island, Hudson Bay, and as far south as Labrador.

Breeding Area

Winter Area

■ Isolated Winter Records

OLDSQUAW

Range of the oldsquaw

Sea Ducks: Their Habits and Habitat

They're not all choosy about their nesting habitat. The hens may lay their eggs, usually from five to seven of them, in open tundra on islands located either offshore or in freshwater lakes, as well as on coastal beaches. There's no telling where they'll pick a site for the nest; it could be far away from other oldsquaws, or it could be in close proximity, as in a colony, to others of their species. Nor do they wait for springtime weather to deposit their eggs. As a general rule, their nests are filled while there is still some ice on the surrounding waterways. The oldsquaw ducklings, soon after they're hatched, are led to the frigid water by their mother. When only half-grown, they head for the sea.

After the oldsquaw hen has laid her eggs, she's faced with problems from hungry predators, such as Arctic foxes, different types of gulls, ravens, and even polar bears. For predatory Arctic animals, an important part of their winter diet is lemmings; when the lemming migration is at low ebb, many ducklings are lost to animal predation. Two-footed predators take their toll, too: Eskimos rob the nests of eggs for food, and utilize the oldsquaw's down, which has the same excellent insulating qualities as eiderdown.

Almost all the oldsquaw's diet consists of crustaceans like shrimp and small crabs. In addition, they feed on mollusks, some aquatic insects, small fish, and fish eggs. Very little plant food has been found in their stomachs, but if a grain ship happens to sink or spill some of its cargo, oldsquaws will feed on that also. I once saw a hundred or so oldsquaws, who, when approached by a boat, seemed so laden with food that they had difficulty getting off the water. They paddled frenziedly a few inches above the surface for about 50 yards before becoming airborne. I believe now that it was a combination of full stomachs and the characteristic of all diving ducks, to churn the water with their webbed feet and flail the air with their wings in order to execute a take-off.

Gunning for Sea Ducks

In mid-September, oldsquaws begin congregating in the Arctic seas, in preparation for their southern migration. About a month later, they have departed the Arctic to spend the winter along the Atlantic coastal areas as far south as North Carolina. Some stay farther north, off the icy coast of Labrador, and many flock to the Great Lakes. Their favorite wintering grounds on the Pacific Coast are southeastern Alaska, Puget Sound, and northern California.

When a New Englander speaks of "coot hunting," the chances are that he's referring to scoters, which are in no way related to the coot. The latter is not a duck, but a black-bodied, white-billed member of the rail family that doesn't even have webbed feet. In most other parts of the country, scoters are referred to by their correct name, although sometimes they're called "scooters," as well as some other crazy nicknames, like Booby, Butter-nose, Tar Bucket, Old Iron Pot, Punkin-blossom Coot, and a host of additional colorful colloquial terms.

Earlier in this book it was explained that there are three varieties of scoters: the whitewing scoter, the surf scoter, and the common scoter, which is also known as the black scoter or the American scoter.

Even the scientists are not in agreement as to the nomenclature of the last-named sea duck. Some of the variations are: *Melanitta nigra americana, Melanitta nigra, Oidemia americana, Oidemia nigra americana,* and just plain *Oidemia nigra.* Take your choice. But to simplify matters, the black, common, or American scoter will hereinafter be known as the common scoter.

The common scoter is all black in its body. The adult male has a touch of color on the base of its bill, a patch of orange that stands out against the stark black of its body. The female is a drab, dark brown, although she has some added cosmetics in the form of a pair of lighter-colored

34

Breeding Area
Winter Area
• Minor Breeding Area

COMMON SCOTER

Range of the common, or black, scoter

cheeks. The feet of the common scoter are another distinguishing feature. They're darkish brown-black, while the feet of the other two scoters are shades of either pink or yellow. The male, weighing about 2½ pounds, averages 19 inches in length, while his mate is somewhat shorter and weighs, on the average, slightly more than 2 pounds.

Powerfully built, in order to withstand the water pressure of considerable depths, with skin like leather and a thick covering of tough, coarse feathers, common scoters use both their feet and wings as they dive for food. They've been found in fishermen's nets at depths of up to 100 feet.

The common scoter, in spite of its name, is the least common of the three kinds of scoters. Because of the shape of its head and bill, the common scoter looks more like a duck than do whitewing and surf scoters. They're not noisy like oldsquaws, but they do sometimes utter a musical whistling sound. They decoy fairly readily and can often be called in by hunters who imitate the sound of their whistling wings in flight. They can fly at about 50 miles per hour or more.

There's no pattern in the way common scoters come in to a rig of decoys. A single may drop in, or maybe a pair; but they may also decoy in groups of up to ten birds, and sometimes in flocks of 25 to 35. Nor is there any uniformity in the way they fly. They could be in V-shaped flights like Canada geese; or they may fly in a wavy line or as an irregular-spaced flock.

Although they congregate along seacoasts, common scoters prefer to feed in the more protected waters of bays and sounds, where there are large quantities of shellfish. Examinations of their stomachs indicate that 90 percent of their diet is mollusks (mussels, clams, oysters, barnacles, and limpets), insects, and small fish. The balance of their food consists of submerged weeds and grasses.

Sea Ducks: Their Habits and Habitat

This species breeds around the coast of Alaska, northern Asia, Newfoundland, Labrador, and northern Europe as far south as Ireland. The female camouflages her nest, which is near tundra ponds and contains from six to eight pink or light-buff-colored eggs. She teaches the ducklings to hide, to dive, and to feed on insects and other foods. While diving for their food, the ducklings sometimes become tired, and the mother carries them on her back while she paddles to shore.

The common scoter is the first type of scoter to leave the nesting grounds and head south, usually about the middle of September. The older birds leave before the young ones, which start to migrate during October. Its wintering territory includes the Atlantic coast from Maine to South Carolina and Georgia, and the Pacific coast as far south as California; some are found also in the Great Lakes during the winter. In other parts of the world, common scoters winter in China, Japan, the British Isles, and the Mediterranean.

Like all sea ducks, the whitewing scoter has acquired many names over the years, both from scientists and from hunters. Also referred to as the American velvet scoter, the whitewing, in scientists' terminology, can be *Melanitta deglandi, Melanitta fusca deglandi*, or *Oidemia deglandi*. (Sometimes it seems as if the main mission in life of avian biologists is to confuse the public, especially writers attempting to present the correct scientific names of certain species.) According to my British friend, Colin Shedden, of the British Association for Shooting and Conservation, whitewings in Europe are a separate subspecies, known as velvet scoters *(Melanitta fusca)*.

Waterfowl hunters can be quite imaginative in naming birds. The whitewing scoter has been called Velvet Scoter,

Gunning for Sea Ducks

Whitewinged Surf Scoter, Bell-tongue Coot, Sea Brant, Sea Horse, White Eye, and other names. My favorite among the colloquial names for this species is Uncle Sam Coot. It would be interesting if a graduate student would base his doctoral thesis on the derivation of some of the nicknames for sea ducks.

Some waterfowl specialists declare the whitewing to be the most abundant of the three different scoters; others claim that surf scoters are the most populous. In any case, whitewings outnumber the common scoters.

The whitewing scoter gets its name logically; the wings of both sexes have prominent white patches, which are more noticeable in flight than when the birds are sitting on the water. They're rugged birds and the largest of the three kinds of scoters. The male, about 21 inches in length, weighs about 3½ pounds, while the length of the 2½-pound female averages 19 inches. The drake has a black body and differs from the female in that his yellow-orange bill terminates in a swollen black bulge, and he has a unique comma-shaped, pure-white patch under his eyes. The female is a muddy brown, with a darker bill and a pair of lighter-colored patches on either side of the head. They both have comparatively short necks and fairly large heads. They can also be distinguished by their feet, which are pink in color.

Whitewings, like other scoters, feed mostly on mollusks—clams, oysters, scallops, and barnacles—crabs, and crayfish. Small fish and aquatic insects account for only a small percentage of their diet. They're not as deep-diving as some of their cousins. They can feed in 40 feet of water and are capable of staying under water for almost a minute, after which they surface for about 12 seconds for breath intake. There are those who believe that a shot-crippled whitewing may dive to the bottom and grasp a patch of seagrass with his bill, staying submerged until he drowns.

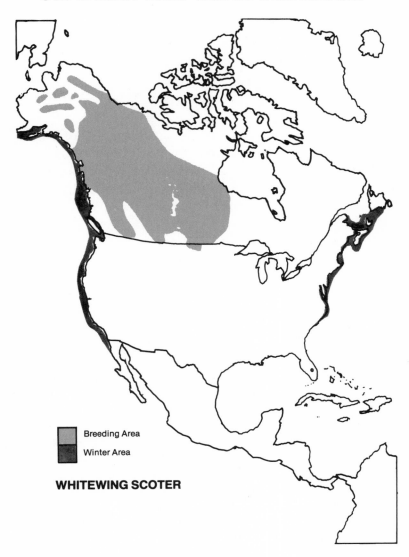

Range of the whitewing scoter

Gunning for Sea Ducks

Aside from a hoarse, croaking voice, the only sound heard from whitewing scoters probably comes from their wingbeats. It has been described as a "bell-like whistle" or the sound of "tinkling ice." The latter description no doubt emanates from a thirsty hunter who is looking forward to a shoreside libation.

The nesting area of the whitewing scoter extends from the northern part of North Dakota, up through central and northwestern Canada, and into lower-central Alaska. Although whitewings are not concentrated in northwestern Alaska, they are found in scattered patches of nesting areas in that region. There is some nesting along the easternmost part of the northern Alaska coast and the northwestern Canadian coast, but the vast majority prefer to locate their nests inland.

Scientists appear to be baffled about the nesting habits of whitewing scoters, because their nests are so difficult to find. Waterfowl researchers seem to disagree about whether whitewings nest near the edges of freshwater lakes, or whether they place their nests several hundred feet from the water. Often, the nests are situated in unusually thick cover, whence it is sometimes difficult for the female to escape when disturbed. The nests, constructed of sticks and leaves, are in small depressions in the ground. Lined with down, they contain from six to 15 pinkish eggs. On the average, only about 75 percent of the eggs survive to hatch, due to predators. Soon after hatching, the ducklings congregate in large groups. Some observers have seen as many as 100 whitewing ducklings in a single group, all of them less than two weeks old.

Because these scoters are comparatively late in establishing their nests, the young birds apparently are not yet strong enough in the early fall to undertake the long migratory flight, even though the adults are ready to head south. It is believed that this accounts for the impatient mature males' leaving a month or so before the females and the young of the year.

Not much is known about the whitewing scoter's migration patterns. Some of them seem to fly without stopping from the breeding areas to their wintering grounds. When migrating, they fly 24 hours a day. At night, they fly over land where possible, but prefer to fly over water during the daylight hours. Also, like other scoters, migrating whitewings stick with their own breed; but after reaching their wintering territory, they flock in with other sea ducks.

Whitewing scoters begin to appear in New England in September, although the large masses don't arrive until about the middle to the latter part of October. On the Chesapeake Bay, the whitewings are the last of the scoters to arrive.

The winter territory of whitewing scoters ranges with fairly uniform distribution along the Atlantic Coast from Newfoundland to North Carolina, with concentrations in the more protected waters of Vineyard Sound, Long Island Sound, Delaware Bay, and Chesapeake Bay. Some of the birds flock into the Great Lakes, and they've been reported in increasing numbers in Nebraska, Colorado, and Louisiana. On the West Coast, they're spread out from the Aleutian Islands south as far as Baja California. Across the Pacific Ocean whitewings winter along the coasts of China and Japan. Like all scoters, the timing of the whitewings' northern migration is later than other ducks. The first to leave are the nonbreeding younger birds, who take off between March and May. The mature birds begin to fly north in large flocks usually about the middle of May.

Of all the scoters, the male surf scoter (*Melanitta perspicillata*) has the most interesting bill and head coloration. The slightly humped, elongated bill has an orange background, with some red around the nostrils, and yellow on the tip;

in the rear part of the bill, there's a large white area, in the center of which is a round black bull's-eye. He has a white cap on the top of his head and a large white patch extending from the back of the head down to the body, which is black. His feet are orange-red. The female has a dirty-brown body and, on the head, a pair of white patches similar to those on a female whitewing scoter. Her feet are yellow or brownish-red. The 19-inch-long surf scoter weighs around 2 pounds, the female being an inch shorter in length and a few ounces lighter in weight. They're not talkative birds, but have been heard clucking and whistling among themselves.

As for their diet, surf scoters feed mostly on clams, mussels, and barnacles. During the summer, they eat aquatic weeds and grasses, seeds, berries, and a considerable amount of aquatic insects.

Their far-north (but subtundra) breeding area begins in Labrador and northeastern Quebec, dodges Hudson Bay, and picks up again in north-central Canada, where it spreads out westward and northward to the upper coast of Alaska.

Waterfowl researchers have found it difficult to get a reliable handle on how numerous surf scoters are compared to the other two scoters, but it is generally believed that their population may exceed the others. Nor is much known about their breeding habits, because they seem to have received a minimum of study by waterfowl experts and ornithologists.

What is known is that their nests are very well camouflaged and are situated in terrain that is difficult for researchers to reach. The few nests that have been observed are in marshes, where they're concealed by the tall surrounding grasses. Made mostly of weeds, the down-lined nest contains from five to nine pinkish or light-buff eggs. In their mating behavior, the coy female is courted by about

Breeding Area
Winter Area

SURF SCOTER

Range of the surf scoter

six drakes, who get a strenuous workout as she dives and tests them to determine which one has the greatest stamina to stay underwater for an extended period.

In September, the mature surf scoters begin to head for their wintering grounds, the younger birds beginning their southward migration a few weeks later. The Pacific Coast birds spend their winters from the Aleutian Islands to Baja California. Some go to the Great Lakes. The Atlantic range of surf scoters extends from Nova Scotia to Florida, predominantly in the coastal and inland waters between New Jersey and Virginia.

The common eider (*Somateria mollissima*) comes in four different varieties, each with its own scientific name. For the sake of simplicity, however, let's forget the distinctions, which are not really important for the purposes of this book. Just for the record, though, the four races are: the American eider, the Pacific eider, the Hudson Bay eider, and the northern eider. Here, we'll treat them all together under the general name, common eider.

These are big birds, in fact, the largest wild ducks in the Northern Hemisphere. They have a chunky body and a short neck, topped with a rather large head, which in the drake is striking in its coloration—tones of yellow, black, white, and green. The common eider is the only duck with a black underbelly and a white back—the drake, that is. The female is not so ostentatious; her head and body are a drab, dark brown, which provides effective camouflage when she's nesting. Also, unlike other female ducks, which have mottled or streaked breasts, she has dark brown bars on her breast and sides.

Weights of the common eider are roughly from 4 to 5 pounds for the male, and generally about a pound less for the female. Their length varies from about 22 inches in the male to slightly less in the female. In flight, they hang their

Range of the common eider

heads, as if their neck muscles are not strong enough to hold the head higher. Although they're deceptively fast-flying birds, they appear to be slow and awkward in the air, because their wingbeats are not as rapid as other ducks'. A unique characteristic of the common eider is its habit of sometimes flapping its wings in flight, then relaxing and soaring. This is the only duck that flies like that.

It's a wonder that the poor common eider has been able to survive at all. For one thing, they're trusting, un-suspicious birds. Their eggs have been picked by Indians and Eskimos as food that keeps for months during the winter. And their down has long been famous as the best insulating material for comforters, clothing, and sleeping bags. While North Americans pillaged the eiders, Euro-peans have shown a commendable and realistic restraint in conserving a valuable natural resource. As a consequence, eiders have not only been protected in Iceland and Scan-dinavian countries, but have been semidomesticated so that the down can be utilized commercially. In Canada, there are eider farms for this purpose.

As the map indicates, the common eider's breeding area covers much of the coastal sections of Siberia, Alaska, Canada, northern Maine, Greenland, and Iceland. In northern Europe, they breed along the Baltic Sea, the coasts of Scandinavia, and the Shetland, Orkney, and Hebrides is-lands off Scotland.

During courtship, while both are on the water, the drake emits a loud call to lure the female and, in order to show off the plumage of his black belly, seems to rise from the water as he assumes an almost vertical position. The female locates her nest close to other nesting eiders and places it among rocks, brush, and tall reeds. The nest, made from nearby materials such as grasses, seaweed, and moss, contains about five greenish-colored eggs.

Sea Ducks: Their Habits and Habitat

The female common eider somehow works her down into a feltlike blanket which extends up the sides of the nest and is used to cover the eggs and insulate them against the intensely cold weather. If the down and the eggs are removed by the down collectors, the female plucks more down from her breast to renew the nest lining, and produces a second clutch of eggs.

Common eiders feed mostly on mussels and other shellfish, which they're capable of swallowing whole, leaving the chewing up to the gravel in their digestive systems. They use both their wings and their feet underwater, but they're not noted for deep diving, though they can go as deep as 40 feet or more, where necessary to get to their food. However, they prefer to feed in the shallows, and are most active during low tide. At night, they raft together on the water or roost on isolated rocks.

During the fall and winter, many common eiders remain in or near their breeding grounds. But on the Atlantic Coast, some venture as far south as Maryland, although major concentrations of them winter along the New England coast and north of there. On the West Coast, the majority stay in Alaska and northern Canada, with a few coming down as far as the state of Washington. In both cases, the common eider prefers coastal waters, and never winters in bays or inland lakes.

Somateria spectabilis, as the scientists call the king eider, could well be the bird that inspired the expression "queer duck." The drake has a weird, concave forehead, orange in color with a black rim around it. The rest of his head has various tones of white, green, and gray, while his chest varies from buff to white. He has a short, orange bill, yellow legs, white wing patches, and a white patch on the lower rump, forward of the tail. Most of his back is black,

Range of the king eider

as is his belly. The female has a grayish bill, and her body is a paler brown, but otherwise she is roughly similar to the female common eider. The drake makes a guttural sound, while some observers have heard him cooing, almost like a mourning dove. The female makes a guttural croak, and hisses and growls if she's disturbed while nesting.

King eiders are large and bulky, measuring and weighing about the same as common eiders. Their feeding habits parallel those of the common eider, but their diet also includes sand dollars and sea urchins. They are known to be good divers, because they've been found entangled in fishermen's nets at depths of 180 feet.

During the breeding season, king eiders are abundant all over the far north. If you happen to be wandering around the polar region—which seems highly unlikely—the chances are you'll stumble across plenty of king eiders, because there are over a million of them up there. As the map reveals, their breeding area covers most of the Arctic—even beyond the top of the map, since they're circumpolar.

Their nesting habits are similar to those of the common eider, except that the females build their nests along the coast or close to ponds in the tundra as well as inland lakes. Sometimes, they place their nests on arid, bare, sloping terrain above lakes and ponds. The architecture of their nests and the number of eggs are also similar to the common eider's.

The king eider's fall migration starts early, usually in August. During migration, they fly in long, straight strings, staying close to the water's surface. They do fly over land, but mostly their flights are over water. Some remain for the winter in the north country, as long as there are unfrozen waters. Many head for the Aleutians, while a fair number swing down the Pacific Coast as far south as Washington. They're found along the shores of the Great Lakes and off the Atlantic Coast down to North Carolina, although only a comparative few migrate that far south. They seem to like reefs and ledges far offshore. Their numbers on the East Coast are not as concentrated as the common eider's winter populations. Along about April, the flights of king eiders head north again, often in huge flocks.

The spectacled eider, *Somateria fischeri*, is another unusual-looking creature. With his goggles that make him resemble an old-time aviator, and his sea-green head and bright-orange bill, the drake is a distinguished-looking bird. Spectacled eiders are distinguished in another way. Depending on which duck authority you accept, he may be known also as *Arctonetta fischeri* or *Lampronetta fischeri*. Either way, Fischer gets into the act; the bird is also known as Fischer's eider, an alternate name which everyone seems to agree on.

Aside from his spectacular head, the drake of this eider type has a white back and a mostly black body; like the king eider, he has the same white patch near his tail. Both sexes have feathers on the rear portion of their bills, which are gray-blue on the female. She also has the spectacled look, although it's more subdued than on the male. Her coloring is brownish, with a barred breast and underside. Both male and female have yellow feet and legs. In size, they're about the same as the king eider, or a bit smaller.

Owing to their remote habitat and relatively limited numbers, not much is known about spectacled eiders. They breed along the western Alaska coast and in northeastern Siberia. During the winter, they seem to go to the Bering Sea, where they disappear, although some move down to the Aleutian Islands.

Spectacled eiders seem to be mute, even in courtship. They're not divers, feeding mostly in the shallows, where they eat aquatic animals, together with a higher percentage of vegetable matter than is consumed by other eiders. For nesting sites, they like small islands off the coast, or inland

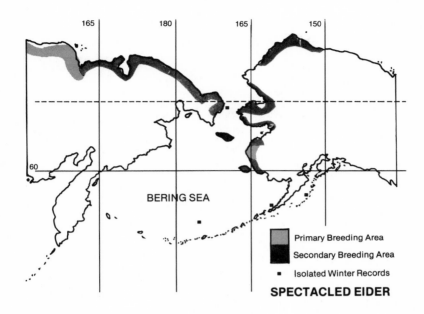

Range of the spectacled eider

ponds and marshes, where the water is either fresh or brackish. The nest, containing about five olive-buff eggs, is in a hollow on the ground or among rocks, and is made of some grasses but with a high proportion of down and feathers.

Although Eskimos have taken a serious toll on spectacled eiders by robbing their nests and beating the flightless, molting birds to death with clubs, their numbers seem to be fairly stable.

Relatively little is known about Steller's eider, *Polysticta stelleri*, mainly because of its limited range and sparse distribution.

Speedier, faster, and much more graceful than the other eiders, the Steller is a smaller bird, weighing under 2 pounds and measuring 18 inches at most. Its rapid wingbeats produce a whistling sound as the ducks fly around in small flocks.

The drake is a handsome, if unusual-looking, duck. His white head is punctuated with a black spot around the eye, and a black collar that extends into a black-and-blue, tapered triangular pattern that goes across the central part of his mostly white back. The large, buff-ginger-colored area on his breast reaches down and back beyond his feet, which are slate colored, as is the bill. He's the only sea duck that can boast of blue-and-white stripes on his wings. The female, with splashes of blue and white on her wings against a rich-brown body, is more colorful than other eider hens.

There are varying opinions as to which male duck is the prettiest to behold. Certainly, the chi-chi wood duck and the mallard, with its iridescent green head, clerical collar, and impudent little curled feather on his lower back are both beautiful birds. However, both species have been so over-used by wildfowl artists and carvers of decorative

Sea Ducks: Their Habits and Habitat

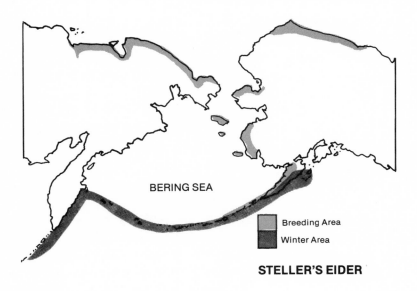

BERING SEA

Breeding Area
Winter Area

STELLER'S EIDER

Range of the Steller's eider

ducks that they have become the clichés of the waterfowl world, rivalled only by the Canada goose and the loon. I happen to like the chiaroscuro effect of the oldsquaw's plumage, and I like the canvasback's streamlined simplicity and rich coloring.

Which brings us to the harlequin duck, whose scientific name, *Histrionicus histrionicus*, is quite appropriate. "Histrionic" is defined in the dictionary as "dramatic or theatrical in manner." The duck's popular name is apt, too, because the dictionary states that a "harlequin" is a clownlike character in multicolored garb. Clownlike they are, and seemingly happy-go-lucky as they cavort and dive and play among themselves, even in the wildest of waters.

The harlequin drake looks as if Mother Nature started out to design an Arctic version of the wood duck, but got bored with the job halfway through the project and abandoned it. Only a color photo or a painting could explain or do justice to the male harlequin's unique color scheme. There are so many mixed-up tints and colors that it's hard to know where to start describing the bird.

The drake's head, for example, has a large, white comma reaching from the lower part of the face, narrowing as it curls up around the eye, and ending on the top of the head, where it meets a reddish-brown stripe running fore and aft. There's a round white spot behind and below the eye, and a long, white vertical stripe behind that. All this is against a dark, slate-blue background. The stubby bill is blue-gray, with a yellowish tip. There's a white, black-rimmed collar at the base of the short neck and a white stripe at the rearmost part of the breast, plus another white stripe running from the front part of the back to the rear, ending at the black fanny. The sides are a reddish chestnut, and there's another circular white spot before the rump begins. To complete the picture—if that's possible—there

The male harlequin sports a unique color scheme.

are several white bars on the wings, and the feet are blue-gray. As I said, a color photo would save a lot of words. The well-known Chinese proverb surely is applicable in this case.

What a relief to describe the dull, colorless female. The only thing that distinguishes her dark-brown and dark-gray form are three light splotches scattered on each side of her face.

Harlequin ducks are fairly small, weighing less than 1½ pounds on the average, and measuring only about 16 or 18 inches from stem to stern. The female calls in a shrill whistle, with several notes, starting higher in pitch, then becoming lower. The male has a deeper, lower call, which is somewhat hoarse.

Their breeding range in the west runs from parts of Alaska, through western Canada, and down into northern California and into parts of the northwestern states. On the Atlantic side, harlequins breed along the northern coast of Canada, parts of Greenland, and in Iceland.

For the winter, harlequins in the west generally don't migrate very far. The Atlantic harlequins hardly change their range in Greenland and Iceland, but on the North American continent, they are concentrated around the coast of Labrador and that region. A few of them may drop into one of the Great Lakes, giving the impression that they're lost. However, they're not really lost; they're simply being characteristically unpredictable. A small fraction of harlequins ventures as far south as New Jersey, and a scattering of singles and pairs has occasionally wandered down to coastal Maryland. Although they are extremely hardy birds, the limits of their southward migration depend on the severity of a particular winter.

For their nest sites, some harlequins like nothing better than hilly regions with snowy peaks and foaming mountain streams. Most of them nest near craggy, rocky

Breeding Area

Winter Area

■ Isolated Winter Records

HARLEQUIN DUCK

Range of the harlequin duck

Gunning for Sea Ducks

shorelines. The nest itself is made of grass, twigs, and leaves, and contains about five eggs.

Their diet, like that of most sea ducks, is based largely on mussels, for which they're capable of diving fairly deep. However, during nesting, if they set up shop near a turbulent mountain stream, their food is more like that of a trout—nymphs of stone flies and mayflies, and the larvae of caddis flies. On inland streams, even when the current is swift, the little harlequins are amazing as they move upstream under the water, both swimming and walking against the rushing current.

As for the overall numbers of harlequins, it seems to be a matter of estimation, but it is believed that there are nearly a million of them.

The adult male harlequin has been described as "fantastically decorated, delightful in color, elegant in form, and graceful in carriage." It's a pity that such an interesting, brilliantly hued bird limits its habitat generally to inhospitable terrain and an unfriendly climate.

4

Where to Go Sea-Duck Shooting

IT'S UNFORTUNATE that the best sea-duck shooting is in a place that's the least accessible to most American gunners—Alaska. And the best shooting there for sea ducks and other ducks, sometimes called "game ducks," is near Homer, Alaska. More specifically, it's in the waters of China Poot Bay, a smaller body of water that's notched into the eastern shoreline of Kachemak Bay. The latter comes off Cook Inlet, near the broad base of the tail-like, curling appendage of the Alaskan panhandle. Both Cook Inlet and Kachemak Bay can be pinpointed on the spectacled eider map in Chapter 3. On the map's grid, check the intersection of the coordinates 60 and 150. Just west-southwest of that point are Cook Inlet and the little indentation that is Kachemak Bay. Both are along the south-central coast of Alaska; as the maps in Chapter 3 indicate, that is a popular wintering area—and in some cases, a breeding area—for sea ducks.

The freshwater and saltwater marshes around Kachemak Bay are the habitat of a vast number of birds during their spring and fall migrations. In addition to ducks, an abundance of sea-, woodland, and water birds are seen in the region. It has been documented that the marine productivity of Kachemak Bay is the richest in North America.

Gunning for Sea Ducks

It's possible that this spot offers the best shooting for ducks in the world. There are at least 20 species available to the gunner. The list includes, among others, mallards, pintails, green-wing teal, and widgeons; the sea ducks that are plentiful there are all three scoters, oldsquaws, Steller's eiders, and common eiders. The daily bag limit is seven regular ducks and 15 sea ducks. There is no figure on how many hunters shoot sea ducks in the state, but a reliable source estimates that it's less than two percent of the limited number of duck hunters in Alaska.

Without question, the best place to shoot sea ducks—and ducks in general—is out of Michael McBride's lodge in Kachemak Bay. Accessible only by boat or float plane, the area around the lodge offers an exciting array of wild fauna and flora that ranges from seals, porpoises, and whales to bald eagles and puffins, and from weasels and marmots to mountain goats and brown bears. McBride is more than the host of an outstanding hunting operation; he is also a noted naturalist and conservationist, having organized the China Poot Bay Society, a nonprofit organization dedicated to the responsible stewardship of Alaskan coastal resources.

Blessed with a climate that usually resists freezing until December, the comfortable McBride lodge has great shooting for sea ducks. Added to that is the fact that this is one of the few places where a waterfowler has a chance of bagging harlequin ducks, which are coveted for the uniquely colored plumage of the drakes, which make handsome mounts when done by a good taxidermist.

The shooting there is not based on the time of day, but depends on the tides, which rise and fall 20 feet, and at the extreme, 30 feet. Most of the blinds are located above the high-tide point, so that in many cases the gunner is shooting down at the birds; but there are also floating blinds—rafts camouflaged with evergreen boughs.

60

Where to Go Sea-Duck Shooting

McBride uses a variety of decoys, but his preference is for the magnum surf scoters made by the Quack Decoy Company. Usually, the sea ducks are so trusting that they fly in close to the decoys and present fairly easy targets. For that reason, McBride suggests that his hunters use No. 4 steel shot as well as No. 2 steel, which is effective on the big whitewing scoters. There is, unfortunately, a problem with recovering cripples, especially oldsquaws and harlequins, which are quickly swept away by the swift tides and which, after being hit, have a habit of coming up and exposing only their bills before diving again. For this reason, it's helpful that the McBride operation includes a kennel of well-trained retrievers who don't hesitate to dive into the foaming waters and bring in the birds.

Because so many eagles feed on the crippled birds, the conservation-minded McBride has for years encouraged his gunners to use steel shot, which is nontoxic and will not pass along any lead poisoning to the eagles. He also has been trying to get ammunition manufacturers to develop shell casings made of biodegradable material, so that the spent shells will not wash in with the tide and litter the shoreline.

Sliding down the Pacific Coast, there doesn't seem to be much sea-ducking until we reach Washington and Oregon; even there the sport does not appear to have caught on in a big way. There is some sea-duck shooting in the Puget Sound area of Washington, and off the coast of Oregon.

Our most populous state entertains during the winter all three varieties of scoters and a few oldsquaws along its coast. However, sea-duckers are apparently about as plentiful in California as are untanned members of the bikinied beach brigade. Although the birds are fairly abundant there, gunners are not much interested in shooting them—

for two reasons. First, other duck species are more available, and, second, the sea ducks congregate in rocky offshore areas, where access is both limited and risky. In fact, Bruce Dewell, a state waterfowl specialist, remarked to me that during his 14 years on the job, he has never heard of anyone hunting sea ducks. Dewell's comment is in direct conflict, though, with an article in one of the major outdoor magazines, which stated that sea-duck hunting is "rapidly expanding" in California.

When we move to the nation's midsection, sea ducks may show up almost anywhere. Though not in substantial numbers, they seem to be spreading southward along the Central and Mississippi flyways. Thus, a few scoters have migrated to unlikely winter habitats such as South Dakota and down into Kentucky. Unusual weather conditions may send sea ducks into virgin territory. Gunners in Nebraska, Kansas, and Colorado have been surprised to see wintering oldsquaws, while the Gulf coasts of Texas and Alabama seem to be harboring increasing numbers of sea ducks; but they're probably wandering strays and are not significant in quantity.

In the Great Lakes states and Canada, interest in sea ducks is low but the sport may be slowly gaining wider acceptance in some areas. In Michigan, where hunting in general is practically a household word, sea ducks are hunted only incidentally by gunners who are primarily after scaup and other diving ducks. If a flight of sea ducks is attracted to a rig of scaup decoys, the shooters will take a crack at them, but it's unheard of for a party to go after sea ducks as their main targets.

That information was provided by a veteran duck hunter, Ed Mikula, who is assistant chief of wildlife in Michigan's Department of Natural Resources. Ed agrees that sea ducks are fine table fare; his suggestion for the preparation of the birds is included in Chapter 7.

Where to Go Sea-Duck Shooting

The U.S. Fish and Wildlife Service estimate for 1986 showed that scoters accounted for only .32 percent of the total ducks harvested in Michigan, while the figure for oldsquaws was a mere .06 percent of the state's duck harvest. Both of those percentages were lower than in 1985, when the figures were .84 percent and .25 percent, respectively.

Of the total ducks bagged in Ohio in 1986, only .96 percent were sea ducks, all of them being scoters. The percentages for the previous year included all three types of sea ducks, and were higher than in 1986: scoters .98 percent, oldsquaws .31 percent, and eiders .13 percent.

Likewise, across the border in Ontario, I'm told that gunners show little interest in sea ducks. According to Ray Stefanfski, provincial wildlife director, the interest in sea ducks in his jurisdiction is, to quote him, "minimal, not worth considering."

The Atlantic seaboard accounts for more sea-duck shooting than any other part of the country, and very likely more than any part of the world. One reason is that New England gunners have been shooting sea ducks for more than 100 years. Another reason is that the Atlantic Flyway is an inviting wintering area for all waterfowl. In addition to geese and other ducks, there's a plenitude of fall and winter sea ducks from Maine down to Long Island, New Jersey, Delaware, Maryland, and, in somewhat diminishing numbers, Virginia and the Carolinas.

That doesn't mean that all species of sea ducks are abundant throughout the northern and central Atlantic Coast. Eiders, for example, are not found in great numbers south of New England. In parts of Long Island, whitewing scoters seem to be the predominating species. Delaware and the Chesapeake Bay are the winter home of oldsquaws and all three types of scoters.

Moreover, the winter populations of East Coast sea ducks are fairly stable, the only variables being summer nesting conditions and disease. The chief reason for the stability of sea duck numbers is the continuing availability of their favorite foods—mollusks and other forms of bottom-dwelling animal life along the seacoast and in the bays bordering the Atlantic Ocean.

By contrast, Canada geese numbers fluctuate due to a combination of breeding success, the availability of their preferred food, and the intensity of gunning pressure. Geese concentrations are subject to alterations in their wintering habitats. For many years, the honkers wintered as far south as Florida, and swarmed into Lake Mattamuskeet in North Carolina. But changing agricultural practices on the Delmarva Peninsula caused the fickle birds to shortstop and spend their winters in the Chesapeake Bay region as well as sections of Delaware. Added to the attraction of fields where the corn was not thoroughly picked up by mechanical harvesters are several national wildlife refuges that are managed for ducks and geese—in Maryland, Blackwater and Eastern Neck Island National Wildlife Refuges, and in Delaware, several coastal refuges, notably Bombay Hook National Wildlife Refuge.

There seems to be a fairly recent trend for Canadas as well as burgeoning numbers of snow geese to winter farther north. Delaware and the upper counties of Maryland's Eastern Shore are the wintering ground of hundreds of thousands of geese, while an increasing number of the birds are spending the fall and winter in Pennsylvania, which has no seacoast but some large freshwater impoundments near productive farmlands.

Sea ducks are more dependable. Instead of being interested in corn-laden fields, they come year after year to their favorite winter resorts, where their underwater sustenance has so far remained stable.

Maine is a good example of this. As stated previously, sea ducks have always been one of the favorite targets of gunners in New England, where for generations sportsmen have been shooting "coots," as scoters are called there. In Maine, black ducks for years have been the primary targets of waterfowlers. With the decline in black-duck numbers, more gunners are shooting sea ducks. While there are plenty of scoters and thousands of oldsquaws along the Maine coast, the area is notable for being part of the eiders' breeding range. That, plus the fact that they're bigger birds, accounts for eiders being the favorites of Down East sea-duckers. In fact, the U.S. Fish and Wildlife Service, in its 1986 waterfowl harvest estimates, found that eiders represent more than 22 percent of all the ducks harvested in Maine.

Eiders were threatened at one time, but thanks to a state conservation program begun in 1965, there are now an estimated 30,000 nesting pairs of eiders along the Maine coast. The result, according to one waterfowl scientist, is that eiders outnumber all forms of waterfowl there.

The abundance of sea ducks and the decline of black ducks are two reasons for the increasing popularity of gunning for these birds in Maine. Another reason is that when the inland lakes and ponds freeze over, there's not much hunting for other waterfowl, and so the serious gunners move to the coastal areas for sea ducks. A final reason for the increase in sea-duck shooting in Maine is the realization that the birds are palatable when properly prepared.

The central part of the Maine coast is the most popular and productive for sea-duckers. Blue Hill Bay, Mt. Desert Island, and other areas not far from Bar Harbor are among the favored spots.

The majority of sea-ducking in Maine is on a do-it-yourself basis, there being few commercial guiding operations. No doubt, the best of these is an organization headquartered at Brooks, near the coast about 50 miles northeast of Augusta. Joe Lucey, who runs the outfit with his chef-partner Brenda Haley, picks up his fly-in clients at the Bangor airport. The food is fabulous, according to those who have gunned there; dinners are ordered in advance and include lobster and other seafood, prime rib, steaks, chops, chicken, turkey, and even homemade pizza. Wild game can be prepared, too, if the sports provide it. With the proper scheduling, hunters can combine sea-duck shooting with hunting for puddle ducks, geese, deer, grouse, woodcock, and snowshoe rabbits.

The sea-duck shooting offered by Joe Lucey is typical of Maine. Gunners take up positions at low tide on small islands, ledges, and bars. It's tricky and potentially dangerous, because of sometimes-fierce winds and tides that can run as much as ten feet. When I asked Joe about the distance of the shots at sea ducks, he said, "Anywhere from maximum range to where you can practically kiss 'em on the cheek."

Biologists Richard S. Stott and David P. Olson have made detailed studies of sea ducks in the coastal areas of New Hampshire and Massachusetts. Although their research was conducted some years ago, it can be assumed that their findings are still generally valid, except for the impact of man-made changes that affect the birds' environment. For example, here's what Stott and Olson had to say in their report, *Sea Duck Populations on the New Hampshire Coastline:*

> These coastal areas are being used at an increasing rate for transportation, power-production sites, and recreation; associated pollution problems such as oil spillage and heated water discharges are common. In addition to threats to or actual changes in the environment from these causes, there is a continuing decline in the productive salt marsh habitats through filling and increased domestic and industrial pollution. These changes and especially the losses in productivity will undoubtedly af-

fect the invertebrate foods and populations of sea ducks. Thus, there is a need for a continued inventory of coastal waterfowl, and their environment.

Stott's and Olson's studies embraced a sea-duck census over three years from 41 observation points along a 21-mile stretch of the New Hampshire and Massachusetts coasts. They found that, among the scoters, whitewings predominated, then surf scoters and a few common scoters. Oldsquaws were observed, but not in great numbers.

The scientists believe that the scoter populations varied in proportion to their vulnerability to hunting. Because common scoters were the most vulnerable, they were the least abundant of the scoters. Whitewings, being the least vulnerable to hunting, were the most numerous, while the numbers of surf scoters were between the other two types, apparently because they were intermediate in terms of their vulnerability.

Long Island waterfowlers have taken a good many sea ducks, but only by chance, when whitewing scoters decoy readily to black-duck rigs. With the scarcity of black ducks, it's possible that sea ducks per se will attract more gunning attention.

In New Jersey, there are fewer than 500 gunners who go after sea ducks, according to state wildlife biologist Fred Ferrigno, whose specialty is migratory waterfowl. Most of the Jersey sea-duck shooters do their gunning in either Delaware Bay or offshore in the Atlantic. They get old-squaws and all three varieties of scoters, the majority of them common scoters.

There are fewer than 50 active sea-duckers in Delaware, says veteran gunner Bill Wise, who added that the state's total bag of sea ducks is less than 1,500 birds. There is some offshore shooting out of Indian River Inlet, but most of the activity is in Delaware Bay. Wise believes that the sea

Gunning for Sea Ducks

ducks in Delaware Bay are transients, using that body of water as a stopover en route to the Maryland coast and the Chesapeake Bay.

In Virginia, sea-duck shooting, compared to some other areas to the north, is still in its infancy. This is not because the birds aren't there, but because gunner interest has not been high, although this situation will probably change if the shooting for other waterfowl continues to deteriorate. There are a few guides working out of the famous coastal town of Chincoteague. Gunning parties are taken out both offshore and in Chincoteague Bay. There, and to the south of Chincoteague, in Wachapreague, another famous sport-fishing port, some gunners take their boats out into the Atlantic and enjoy good sea-duck shooting, but as of the 1987-88 season, sea-ducking has not attracted sportsmen in hordes.

Sea-duck shooting has only recently started to catch on in North Carolina and is still not a big deal there. There are no longer any geese to amount to anything, although there is some good, if spotty, duck hunting. One Tarheel gunner, who has access to a choice spot, reported that it's a simple matter to collect a limit of pintails in an hour. (I'll have to see that to believe it.) But, since the goose hunting is practically nonexistent, the guides have become interested in taking out parties for sea ducks. Because it's a comparatively new sporting activity in North Carolina, the outfitters have been uncertain as to how to go about sea-ducking. One of them, Vernon Barrington, went north in 1987, to spend some time learning the best techniques from a veteran Chesapeake Bay guide. As sea ducks seem to be extending their winter range and the guides learn more about getting good shooting for their clients, North Carolina holds promise for more interest in sea-duck shooting.

68

Where to Go Sea-Duck Shooting

Winging back north to Maryland, I hesitate—for fear of being accused of chauvinism—to dwell at length on sea-ducking there. But I feel that extensive coverage of the Chesapeake Bay is in order, for three reasons. First, it's where I've done most of my sea-ducking and can therefore comment on it with a degree of authority owing to firsthand experience as well as some expertise acquired over two decades. Second, it's probably the area where techniques for hunting sea ducks have become most refined over the last 15 years. Finally, considering that it's relatively close to the most populous region in the United States, the Chesapeake Bay offers the best sea-duck gunning to the most people.

There are plenty of sea ducks in the Maryland portion of the Atlantic Ocean, but most smart gunners are not willing to brave the stormy, wintry offshore waters. There's not much point in enduring the hazards and hardships of the ocean, when a few miles to the west of the Delmarva Peninsula lies the Chesapeake Bay. The Chesapeake is the nation's largest estuary and, though sheltered somewhat, is still capable of producing some rough, frothy seas.

There are more professional guides and well-equipped outfitters operating on the Chesapeake than in other winter habitats of sea ducks. Also, there are more sea-duck gunners, many of them locals but perhaps the majority coming from nearby states as well as from distant states, including some from the Great Lakes area. Because of the growing interest of gunners in the sport of sea-duck shooting, there's more competition on the part of the Chesapeake guides. The better ones strive to become more knowledgeable each year, while improving their equipment and technique.

Many of the out-of-state sea-duck gunners are initially attracted to Maryland's Eastern Shore because of its reputation for superb goose hunting. While they're in the area, they try a waterfowl sport that's new to them, and become intrigued with the fast, challenging shooting associated with sea-ducking. Several savvy commercial operators offer a package deal—goose hunting in the morning and sea-duck shooting in the afternoon. It's a good proposition either way. If the geese are flying well, the sports collect their limits early, relax during the lunch hour, then heat up their gun barrels by shooting at sea ducks, which are generally obliging enough to provide action in the afternoon. On the other hand, if the morning goose chase is unproductive, the gunners can almost assuredly get plenty of shooting at sea ducks after lunch, so that their gunning day is not a total loss.

The common scoters are the first arrivals, usually at the end of September and early October. Surf scoters move in a few weeks later. Both of those scoters are believed to migrate down the coastline until they come to the mouth of the Chesapeake, where they swing a bit to the west, then head due north to spend the winter in the middle and upper parts of the Bay. Whitewing scoters move in next; apparently they shortcut the coastline and migrate directly from their far-north breeding grounds to their wintering area in the central Bay. Oldsquaws are the last to appear. The peak period in the Chesapeake is usually the middle of November.

It's neither possible nor practical to list all the Chesapeake sea-duck guides here, because new ones seem to be entering the field each year, while some fly-by-nights drop out. The best source for up-to-date information on this score are Eastern Shore gun shops and sporting-goods stores in Easton, Cambridge, and Chestertown. Sportsmen who are unfamiliar with the scene, after getting the names and phone numbers of several guides and outfitters, should contact them for their current rates and available open dates on their calendars. It's a good idea to ask for references from

70

At the end of a successful sea-duck shoot, Tilghman guide Randolph Murphy, *right*, discusses the hunt with his clients.

satisfied clients, then follow up by contacting them for their opinions.

The outfit run by Norm Haddaway and Leonard Falcone was dealt with in the second chapter. Another experienced sea-duck guide with whom I'm familiar is Randolph Murphy, also based in Tilghman. Although, like most Chesapeake Bay guides, they offer no overnight accommodations, they can put visiting gunners in touch with local hostelries.

A third operation, also in Tilghman, is both a country inn and a famous headquarters for sportfishing and gunning in the Bay. The sea-duck operation is the responsibility of Chuck Harrison, one of the sons of Levin "Buddy" Harrison III, who runs what is reputedly the nation's largest privately owned charter-fishing fleet.

Chuck has taken out about 50 gunning parties during each of the past couple of sea-duck seasons. Most of them took advantage of the Harrison organization's unique package deal consisting of a night's lodging, enough seafood-dominated meals to sink a tugboat, and a sortie after sea ducks.

According to Chuck Harrison's records, about half of his sea-ducking clients were "local," by which he means gunners who come from an 80-mile radius. That includes the greater Baltimore area and the Washington, D.C., area, which takes in part of Maryland and northern Virginia. The other 50 percent of his gunners were largely from Pennsylvania. Most of them were so satisfied that, before leaving, they booked reservations for the next year.

About 60 percent of Harrison's gunners were new to the sea-duck game, and the majority of them were able to bag only about half of the seven-bird limit. In Chuck's experience, a novice sea-ducker requires at least five boxes of shells to bring in a limit, while a gunner who is more or less a veteran at this different type of waterfowling can get by

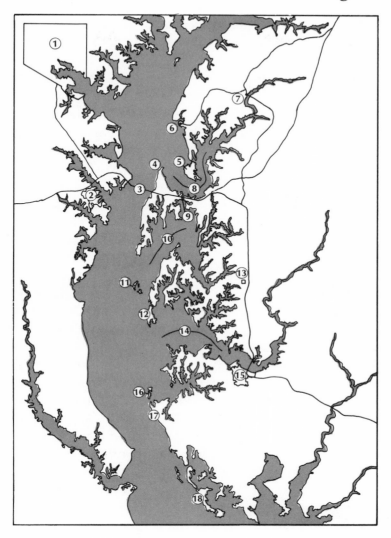

The Chesapeake Bay and points of interest: *1*, Baltimore; *2*, Annapolis; *3*, Bay Bridge; *4*, Love Point; *5*, Eastern Neck Island National Wildlife Refuge; *6*, Rock Hall; *7*, Chestertown; *8*, Chester River; *9*, Kent Narrows; *10*, Eastern Bay; *11*, Poplar Island (3 islands); *12*, Tilghman Island; *13*, Easton; *14*, Choptank River; *15*, Cambridge; *16*, James Island; *17*, Taylors Island; *18*, Hooper Island.

with three boxes. That's 75 shells for seven ducks. No wonder one of his novice clients said, "I never knew a duck could fly that fast."

Bob Haddaway is another commercial sea-duck outfitter operating out of Tilghman. Most of his hunters come from the Carolinas, but an increasing number of New Englanders book hunts with him. Sometimes, when he takes out different parties in the morning and afternoon, both groups bag their limits—which proves again that the time of day is not necessarily a success factor in sea-ducking. Bob Haddaway's log shows that his clients took over 1,200 sea ducks during the 1987-88 season. His rates are based on a policy of "guaranteed shooting or your money back."

While the Chesapeake Bay's Poplar Island area is preferred by sea-duck guides operating out of Tilghman, several outfitters are based a bit to the north. One of them, Richard L. Manning, is from Chestertown but keeps his boat at Kent Narrows. From there, Manning and his sons can easily reach the mouth of the Chester River to the north, or Eastern Bay to the south. Most of his clients are Marylanders from the other side of the Chesapeake, but he has some parties from Pennsylvania and New Jersey, and some from as far away as Minnesota and Utah. Like most of the other guides, Manning also offers hunting for Canada geese.

To the south of Tilghman, the Taylors Island-James Island-Hooper Island section of the Eastern Shore attracts guides and independent sea-duckers from the Cambridge area. There are not many commercial guides around there, but the most prominent is W. D. Wheatley, who's been at it for about six years. Although his hunting lodge is located near the inland town of East New Market, Wheatley takes his gunners out in the Bay near Taylors Island. He gets all three types of scoters, mostly whitewings, with oldsquaws moving in later in the season.

Although this properly belongs in Chapter 7, there's no harm in jumping the gun a bit and stating that W. D. Wheatley is a firm believer in the edibility of sea ducks. His favorite recipe involves soaking filleted sea-duck breasts in buttermilk overnight, then sautéing them. He recently served them that way to a party from Long Island. One member of the group was so impressed with the quality of the game meat that he asked what kind it was. When told that he was eating whitewing scoters, the Long Islander exclaimed, "Well, I'll be damned. This is so good—and for years we've been throwing these ducks away."

And now, migrating across the Atlantic Ocean, we find that, although the better-known duck species attract thousands of British waterfowlers, there's very little sea-duck shooting in the United Kingdom (England, Wales, Scotland, and Northern Ireland). The Wildlife and Countryside Act of 1981 affords protection to any eiders, scoters, and oldsquaws that may venture inland to lakes and rivers. And in the coastal waters, gunners shoot the odd sea duck only when other ducks are the primary quarry.

Denmark—the land that's famous for Hamlet, pastries, and great canines—accounts for most of the sea ducks shot in Europe, although the annual kill there has declined drastically in recent years.

There are thousands of common scoters in Danish waters from September to late March and mid-April. The majority of them favor open waters far from the coast, but they occasionally seek sheltered waters. Following gale-force storms, small flocks have been seen in brackish fiords and even in freshwater lakes.

According to the 1979 figures compiled by Danish waterfowl researcher Ib Clausager, about 20,000 common scoters were bagged in his country that year, most of them by a few expert sea-duck hunters. But there's a different picture in the 1986 *Status of European Quarry Species*, by Colin B. Shedden, an official of The British Association for Shooting and Conservation. The drop in the annual common scoter kill to less than 10,000 seems to be due to the difficulty of hunting them when they stay far out to sea, and because of oil spills: Some years ago, about 7,000 common scoters were lost as a result of oil spillage. Another reason for the decline is that, although there is no bag limit and the birds can be legally hunted for the market, lowered prices and higher freight charges have reduced the number sold to game dealers.

From late October to early May, many thousands of whitewing scoters congregate in Danish waters, but the kill of these birds has decreased from 10,000 to 4,000. The reasons for the lowered harvest are the same as for common scoters.

Danish gunners usually don't shoot many oldsquaws until December or January, when the main flocks arrive in the Baltic Sea. Where some 10,000 oldsquaws were shot annually, in recent years the kill has been less than 7,000.

At one time, 180,000 common eiders were shot each year in Denmark, but now, as pointed out in Shedden's *Status of European Quarry Species*, only about 146,000 of the big sea ducks are bagged, most of them near the islands and in the Baltic Sea.

Outside of Denmark, a relatively small number of sea ducks are bagged by waterfowlers in most of the other countries in the north of Europe, as well as a few hundred off the coasts of the Iberian Peninsula.

For most of us, the U.S.S.R. seems to be on the other side of the world, both geographically and ideologically; but sea ducks, like polar bears, are circumpolar and are not confronted with a white curtain separating them from the communist world. While we know there are sea ducks in Russian and Chinese territory, nothing is known about the shooting of the birds there.

Among the 30-odd American travel agencies specializing in booking hunts in exotic lands, only two have connections for setting up sportsmen's trips to Mongolia, China, and Russia. Their clients are wealthy hunters who are attracted to those countries by big-game species that are not found elsewhere. It's most unlikely that any American waterfowlers would want to try sea-ducking in Asia; there's no incentive for gunners to travel that far in order to enjoy sport that's available here.

CHAPTER **5**

How to Go About Sea-Duck Gunning

THERE ARE three options for those sportsmen who want to try sea-duck shooting for the first time. You can attempt it on your own, you can go out with a friend who has gained some expertise in this special kind of waterfowling, or you can engage a commercial guide.

In that last category, professional guides are not found everywhere that sea ducks are found. Some of them are covered in Chapter 4. As a newcomer to the sport, book a hunt, if you possibly can, with an experienced guide. Even if you plan eventually to shoot independently, it's smart to learn the ropes from a pro.

But first, check out the guide's credentials. Ask him for the names, addresses, and phone numbers of two or three of his customers. Then follow up by contacting those hunters. Ask them if they're satisfied with the guide, although that may seem like a silly question, since the guide wouldn't give you the name of an unsatisfied client. Also inquire about the guide's equipment—his decoys and the comfort and seaworthiness of his boat.

For a gunner who wants to hunt sea ducks independently, it's important to bear in mind the locale. As you no doubt recall from previous chapters, different parts of the country call for different approaches. A hunting procedure that works in coastal Maine is not applicable to Lake Michigan or Delaware Bay.

Aside from Maine and Alaska, the most commonly accepted method is to operate from a boat surrounded by a bunch of decoys. Usually, the boat is self- propelled, but in some areas it's customary for a larger boat to tow a smaller one. When the hunting area is reached, the gunners hop into the smaller boat, which is then anchored. The outfitter deploys his decoys around the anchored craft and moves the main boat some distance away, perhaps a half-mile or less, where he anchors and watches the gunners, while listening for their shots. After a predetermined interval—say, one hour—the mother boat comes back to the hunters and picks up any birds they've shot. On waters where there are strong winds and/or strong tides, the mother boat returns immediately after some shooting is heard. That's because if the big boat doesn't come promptly after the gunfire, the dead ducks may be washed away. Also, in the event of crippled birds, the mother boat can track them down and dispatch them. If the gunners have no action after an hour or so and the outlook is unpromising, the skipper may pick up the decoys and tow the hunting boat to a more likely spot.

I've been on several sea-duck shoots where that tactic was used. It worked out fine, with one exception: The guide heard a volley of shots and brought the big boat to the smaller one, only to find that the embarrassed gunners had wasted about a dozen shells and there were no ducks to pick up.

The above-mentioned exception was a further embarrassment not only because it was the only time I've been skunked on a sea-duck shoot, but also because I had a guest who had come all the way from California to gun the Chesapeake Bay. He had entertained me a year before on a goat hunt on Catalina Island. After hearing me rave about

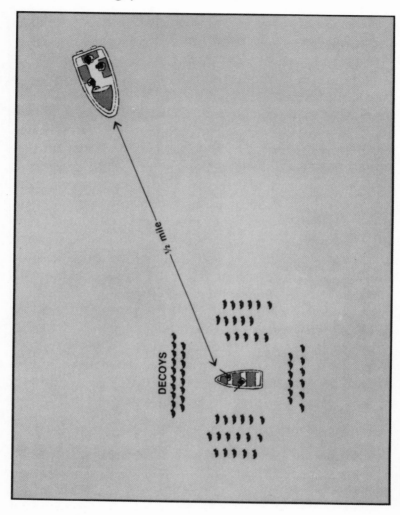

Here, the gunners are dropped off in a small boat, while the mother boat waits in the distance.

the fast action you can expect on a sea-duck shoot, Jim decided to come East and give it a try. On our guided sea-duck hunt, we didn't get a single bird, but the following morning, gunning from a shore blind, we bagged our limits of Canada geese. So, his cross-country trip was not unproductive. I learned some years later that Jim had been the first husband of a much-married movie star, the blonde sex-goddess who did herself in with an overdose of pills.

One professional guide I know uses the mother-boat method, but with a pair of anchored smaller boats, each containing up to four gunners. The boats are moored in about 20 feet of water, far enough apart that they're well out of shotgun range of one another. Between the two gunners' boats is a spread of about 150 decoys. The guide has been using this system for a number of years and both he and his clients are happy with the results.

For the first-timer, it's difficult to lay down any hard-and-fast rules about a boat for sea-duck shooting. The important things are that it's seaworthy, that its power source is dependable, and that you know how to handle it. Safety, of course, should be a prime consideration. A sea-ducking friend of mine won't take out his small boat when the wind is blowing over ten knots. Coast Guard-approved flotation devices, the euphemism for life vests, are a must. Some commercial operators take out liability insurance, in case a hunter slips on a wet deck, is injured, and later files a lawsuit.

Veteran sea-duckers are not in agreement about the coloration of their boats. There are those who believe that a white craft, even on a bright, sunny day, will not scare sea ducks. Others insist that the boat must be painted a dull gray, and a few go so far as to say that the boat should be partly camouflaged, with no visible brightwork. In my opinion, which is based on personal experience combined with extensive brain-picking of numerous experts, it depends on the locale of the sea-duck shoot. In bodies of

Gunning for Sea Ducks

In the early part of the season, it's possible to lure sea ducks with one-gallon plastic jugs, painted flat black with dabs of white to simulate a whitewing scoter.

water where the birds are heavily hunted, they're not as easy to deceive as in sparsely gunned waters. So, the less conspicuous the craft, the better the shooting is.

The degree of gunning pressure is a factor also in the selection of decoys for sea-ducking. In the early days of sea-duck shooting on the Chesapeake Bay, it was possible to attract the ducks with about 50 plastic one-gallon jugs, painted dull black with a few dabs of white, to simulate a flock of whitewing scoters. But now, in the same waters, most knowledgeable guides use 100 full-bodied decoys. This is not only because the birds are wiser than before, but also because there are more sea-duck rigs operating in a popular area, and the boat that's surrounded by the most realistic decoys is the one that gets the most action. Some sea-duckers find they can use the jugs in the early season, but when the ducks become educated after being shot at, they're too wary to come into anything but a spread of real-looking decoys. One sea-ducking friend of mine started out with jugs some years ago, then switched to silhouette decoys mounted on vee-boards. But now, with more boats competing in one large section of water, he uses two dozen full-bodied scaup decoys. When conditions are right, he found, common scoters often decoy in flocks of 50 to 100, while whitewings pop in singly or in pairs or, at most, six in one group.

In a typical sea-duck layout by a professional guide, a dozen or more of the 'coys are tied to a length of heavy line, secured in water by a heavy anchor. Multiple strings, totalling a hundred or more decoys, are bulky and are stowed in large heavy-gauge plastic drums. For this reason, the boat must be large and roomy.

An effective method of deploying the blocks is to put at least three strings on either side of the boat. Astern, there's a tightly packed bunch of decoys, representing a raft of resting ducks.

As for the decoys themselves, there aren't too many manufacturers turning out sea ducks at this writing. To my knowledge, only one firm offers oldsquaw decoys, with their unique long tails. Eider decoys are available from L.L. Bean and others, while scaup decoys—to be repainted or used as is—are commonplace. Those are all made of plastic. But there's nothing like a return to the romance of old-time duck shooting over hand-carved wooden decoys, even though they're relatively more expensive and aren't easy to come by. Whether they're more effective, I can't say, but, aesthetically, it's more pleasing for me to shoot over a rig of hand-carved blocks than it is to shoot over a bunch of plastic factory jobs.

So now, you have your boat and your decoys and your enthusiasm. Where, precisely, should you go? By talking to experienced sea-duckers and a few commercial guides as well as the local state and federal waterfowl specialists, you

A proper sea-ducking boat must be fairly large to accommodate these drums that hold 100 or more decoys.

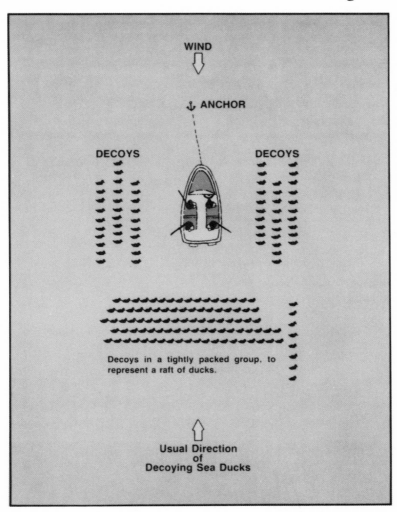

A popular spread for a sea-ducking rig

A pair of plastic oldsquaw decoys

A hand-carved oldsquaw

can get a line on the general area for your attack on sea ducks. To pinpoint the scene of your shoot, you should shake down your boat and at the same time locate the favorite feeding grounds of the birds. When the season is well under way, you should be able to find large concentrations of them. As you cruise the area, use your binocular to spot them in the distance. Without getting too close to the ducks, toss over the anchor, set out your spread of decoys, and be ready for action at any time.

If your decoys look somewhat like the real thing, it shouldn't take long for some of the curious, gregarious birds to come in and look you over. In fact, it's not unusual for them to buzz your boat even before all the decoys are positioned.

If the flying ducks are out of range, you can try calling them. It's not necessary to try to duplicate the call of a sea duck. An ordinary duck call often attracts them. They seem to come to the call more out of curiosity than from a belief that a real duck is speaking to them.

Another trick that sometimes fools sea ducks—especially early in the season—is known as "waving," a practice that many goose hunters use effectively. You can wave any bright-colored object—a handkerchief or even your hunting cap—anything to get their attention and make them want to come in and investigate.

In some waters, it's possible to combine a bit of angling with your sea-duck hunting. I know this is done by some New Jersey sportsmen in Delaware Bay. It's not smart, however, for all hands on board to try catching a fish dinner. While other members of the party are fishing, one person should be clutching his shotgun instead of a fishing rod. That way, when some ducks fly in unexpectedly, at least one person is ready for them, while the others drop their rods and scramble to grab their guns.

A common scoter decoy. Note anchor around neck and weighted keel for stability.

A solid wood surf scoter decoy

6

Armament and Shooting

AT THIS particular time in the history of waterfowling, when starting a chapter with a title such as this one has, it's imperative to deal first with the most controversial issue in the waterfowl world today: steel shot. To start this chapter with any other element in the sport is like kicking off a major meal with dessert. The first course may have been tasty, but the nutritious part of the meal is the meat and vegetables course.

Certainly, the weaponry used on a sea-duck shoot is a matter of vital importance, but the fodder that goes into and out of a shotgun provides the protein, the *sine qua non*, whether we're dealing with a well-balanced dinner or a productive shoot.

To continue the culinary analogy, the steel-shot issue is a hot potato, a subject which must be handled cautiously and with delicacy by a commentator. It's highly subjective in some ways and is fraught with a gamebag-full of personal opinions, some of which are sound, some of which are the result of pure hardheadedness, and some of which are based on ratiocination. There is, however, one inescapable fact: Whether we like it or not, whether or not it accomplishes its goal, we waterfowlers are stuck with steel shot. It's imperative, then, that we learn how to live with this new diet.

Gunning for Sea Ducks

To review briefly the reasons for steel shot being mandatory in most if not all jurisdictions, it all began when waterfowl biologists and game managers became concerned about lead poisoning in ducks and geese. In heavily gunned waters and fields, the accumulated spent lead pellets were ingested by the feeding fowl, many of which ended up deader than if they'd been shot in the head with a load of BBs from a full-choke 10-gauge shotgun from a range of ten yards. Studies of duck gizzards collected nationwide resulted in a conservative estimate that about three million waterfowl were dying annually from lead poisoning, or close to three percent of the wintering population of all waterfowl species.

Not only that, but bald eagles, considered an endangered species in most states, have been affected as well. Feeding on dead or crippled ducks and geese that had lead pellets in their flesh or intestinal tract, the eagles, too, succumbed to lead poisoning. The U.S. Fish and Wildlife Service found that in 1984 alone, 25 bald eagles died from lead poisoning.

As far back as the late 1950s, waterfowl biologists began searching for an alternative to lead shot, one that would be ballistically sound and at the same time nontoxic to waterfowl. Many different metals were tried and field-tested. Steel emerged as the most practical. (An interesting sidelight in the research for a lead-shot substitute is the fact that the ideal metal turned out to be none other than gold, which obviously would be impractical, except for a shotgun-toting Arab oil baron.)

In my state, steel shot was mandatory for one season about 12 years ago, but, under pressure from gunners and their representatives in the legislature, the law was changed back to lead shot. Steel shot, in a much-improved version, was required for the 1987-88 season on all waterfowl, to be phased in nationally within two years. Following that session, reactions from commercial guides and waterfowl shooters were, according to my own informal survey, mixed. About half of those questioned didn't like the new ammo, to put it mildly. About 25 percent said it didn't make much difference, and another 25 percent reported that it was quite satisfactory. The latter two groups agreed that good gunners and those who had taken the trouble to learn how to use steel shot bagged as many ducks with steel as with lead. In essence, the better marksmen and those who confined their shots to reasonable ranges, and people who had learned the performance of steel shot and its limitations, were able to splash their share of ducks.

Some of those I talked to are folks whose integrity I respect. They told me of cases where you could hear the shot hitting the flying ducks, which then flew on, apparently unruffled. And there were stories—which I believe—of low-flying ducks, even though they could be seen centered in the shot pattern on the water, continuing their flight. Without seeming to defend steel shot, I must say that I've seen the same things happen when the guns were belching lead pellets. With any kind of shot, sea ducks are tough, hard-to-kill birds that can take a heap of punishment. Overlying their tough hide is an almost bulletproof coat of heavy, dense feathers and down. One outfitter told me the ducks were easier to bring down in the first part of the season, but with the advent of cold weather their bodies put on an extra layer of down, making them harder to kill. That may or may not be an old guides' tale.

Among the many objections to steel shot, the chief ones are:

1. The reports of lead poisoning in waterfowl are exaggerated. Nobody sees those dead ducks and geese that allegedly died from lead poisoning.

2. Being a harder metal than lead, steel pellets damage shotgun barrels.
3. Steel shot is not as effective as lead shot, because it cripples more birds than it kills.
4. Steel shotshells are more expensive than lead shot.
5. Those who load their own shells will be forced to buy the more costly factory ammunition.

Waterfowl biologists, responsible conservation organizations, game-management professionals, most of the informed gunning experts, and ammo manufacturers (who originally resisted the switch to steel because of the problems of retooling) counter the objections as follows:

1. Lead-poisoned fowl don't remain out in the open for everyone to see. Instead, they conceal themselves in dense cover, to try to avoid predators and scavengers, which eventually consume them.
2. It is true that older shotguns may show barrel damage after the shooting of many rounds of steel shot. It's advisable not to use a treasured older gun on waterfowl. Save it for quail and other forms of upland game. If it's a fairly new gun, there should be no problem with barrel wear or the opening up of the choke. If in doubt, check with the gun manufacturer, giving the model and serial numbers.
3. According to the best shotgun authorities, who have shot, in the aggregate, more than 100,000 rounds of steel loads at ducks and geese, steel shot can be deadly if handled correctly (more on that later).
4. In general, steel shotshells do indeed cost more than lead in waterfowl loads. However, with the increased demand caused by the compulsory use of steel shot on waterfowl, it's reasonable to expect

that better manufacturing methods and more competition will result in lower prices for steel shot.
5. Special handloading components and techniques are
now available for steel shot, making it possible for
the do-it-yourselfer to make steel shotshells for
about half the cost of factory loads.

To handle steel shot effectively, we're advised, it's imperative to make some alterations in our shooting proce-
dures. Just as you can't drive an eighteen-wheel tractor trailer
the same way you'd spin along the highway in a light, four-
cylinder pickup, you must make some adjustments when
switching from lead shot to steel. There are certain guidelines
that are recommended by those who should know.

By now, it's pretty much common knowledge that you
should go two sizes larger in the transition from lead to
steel. For example, if you've been accustomed to shooting
No. 4 lead on ducks, it's advised that, when using steel
shot, you should shoot No. 2's. Steel pellets, being lighter
than lead, must be larger in order to produce the same bal-
listic performance. At the same time, there are more of the
little balls in one ounce of steel shot than in lead. In a one-
ounce load of No. 2 steel shot, there are about 125 pellets,
as opposed to about 87 pellets in No. 2 lead. (Whenever I
hear that, I picture some poor little old Dickensian codger
in a munitions factory, counting pellets: "One hundred and
one, one hundred and two . . .")

The lighter steel pellets have a somewhat higher
muzzle velocity, but tend to decrease in speed over greater
distances. What this means in practical terms is that it's advisable to adjust your *lead* (I've used italics here to distin-
guish the technique from the metal). So, at 30 yards or
under, according to the experts, you should allow less *lead*
with steel than with lead. Between 30 and 50 yards, the sug-

Gunning for Sea Ducks

gested *lead* is the same. Beyond 50 yards, you should hold your fire, because that's where the crippling rate is highest; but if you insist, you should slap plenty of *lead* on those longer shots. (I'll deal with *lead* and range estimation a few pages hereinafter.)

Another factor to be considered is pellet penetration of steel vis-à-vis lead shot. The harder steel pellets are capable of going through more flesh and bone. That explains why the 1988 season evoked numerous comments about more bleeding in slain waterfowl than was the case in the past. Also, lead pellets become microscopically deformed going through the shotgun; in their less-than-round shape, lead pellets are not ballistically ideal.

When further comparing lead and steel shot, it's important to bear in mind the different shot strings produced by the two loads. For those unfamiliar with the term, the shot string is the length of the shot column as it moves from the gun to the bird. The steel shot string is more bunched up, or denser, than the more spread-out, or dispersed, lead shot string. With lead shot, the shot string is about one-third longer than the tighter steel shot string. The result, according to reliable studies, is that steel shot requires greater shooting accuracy; but when the shot is on the mark, more pellets will strike the bird. To put it another way, sloppy shooting with steel shot may mean a clean miss, but a direct hit should result in a clean kill. That's what "reliable studies" indicate; your results from shooting at ducks, and mine, may be different.

Another change is recommended when switching from lead to steel shot: Use a more open choke. There are plenty of gunners who claim they're getting good steel-shot results with a full-choke barrel, and I don't doubt them. The majority of authoritative opinion, however, favors improved cylinder or improved modified for ducks within reasonable ranges—up to 45 yards. The thinking there is based on the fact that steel shot from an improved bore offers roughly the same pattern density as lead shot fired from a full choke.

Here are a final few words about steel versus lead shot. If, after several seasons of evaluating the effectiveness of steel shot, there is definite evidence that steel loads are causing inordinate crippling losses of waterfowl, there's no question in my mind that wildlife authorities and law-makers would reverse themselves and support a change back to lead loads. That eventuality seems doubtful, however, because two things are likely: 1) Gunners will school themselves to use steel shot with telling effect, and 2) ammo makers will continue their research and development of more effective steel shotshells. It's the great free enterprise system in action. Company X strives to turn out a better product than that of Company Y, at a better price. And the public benefits.

The respected National Wildlife Federation, an early champion of steel shot, has stated,

> Years from now waterfowl hunters will look back and wonder what the debate and conflict over steel shot were all about. As documentation of the scope and magnitude of the lead poisoning problem continues to build, and as more and more people interested in wildlife conservation learn about the issue, increasing pressure will be brought to bear on state and federal management agencies to resolve the lead shot problem. Once the dust has settled and the recriminations have ended, steel shot proponents will be looked to and recognized as conservationists who were bold enough to speak out for the resource. Most im-portantly, however, they will have helped to eliminate— once and for all—the needless loss of waterfowl, bald eagles, and other wildlife to lead poisoning.

Gunning for Sea Ducks

And, to quote Jim Carmichel, shooting editor of *Outdoor Life*,

> The best thing we've learned about steel shot is that it kills ducks and geese very nicely. Some folks still say steel shot is no good, but I've noticed that the guys who complain the loudest can't hit ducks with lead shot, either. Over the past dozen years, I've fired hundreds of steel-shot loads at ducks and geese and I've watched thousands more being fired by other hunters. Theoretically, steel shot shouldn't kill as far as lead but, in actual hunting circumstances, they perform about equally well. This is because at ranges of 60 yards and beyond, where lead has the advantage, nine out of ten hunters can't make consistent hits with any kind of shot.

To conclude this discussion of the sea-ducker's artillery, it must be stated that at the time of this writing the sporting-arms industry is in a state of flux, because of the mandatory use of steel shot for waterfowl. Only recently, new 10-gauge pumpguns and autoloaders have been introduced. New over-bored barrel designs are now available, made especially for steel loads. But the most important innovation of all has been the introduction of 3½-inch shotgun shells, loaded with steel pellets, and guns chambered for the 3½-inch biggies, as is a new 12-gauge over-and-under.

In any event, a duck hunter owes it to his sport to be as proficient as he possibly can in gun handling. With the exception of a few well-coordinated gunners, the average duck hunter is not capable of making deadly shots on a consistent basis unless he logs considerable time in preseason practice shooting. One well-known, well-publicized expert on waterfowl shooting states that the average shotgunner is a lousy shot who wounds about 20 percent of the birds he throws pellets at. He may be right, but I suspect he's low by about ten percent.

There are far too many once-a-year gunners—those who dust off their fowling pieces the night before opening day, after not having fired a round since the end of the previous season. When they blaze away at a flock of ducks, it's to be expected that they'll collect their limits of holes in the fall sky. So, they laugh off their misses and say something like, "Gee, I'm really out of practice," or, "That 30-mile wind sure throws your shots off the mark."

That was a few years ago, during the lead-shot era. But now that they're compelled to use steel shot, they have an easy scapegoat for their inferior marksmanship. A shot may be two feet under a duck and three feet behind it, and they say, "It's the fault of that damned steel shot. If I'd been using lead shotshells, that bird would be down and out." That applies to some good marksmen, too. Even the most skilled scattergunners blow a shot occasionally. Because they have a hotshot reputation, they're the first ones to blame a miss on the ammunition—steel shot, in this case.

There are several good ways to burn some powder and enrich the ammo manufacturers, while sharpening up the old shooting eye. Skeet and trap shooting help to build—or destroy—your shotgunning confidence. The newer game of sporting clays, which came to us from Britain, helps develop fast gun handling in the field, although it's more suitable for upland-bird practice than for sea-ducking. For my money, you can't beat shooting at clay birds thrown from a hand trap. You can direct the thrower to concentrate on your weaknesses, whether they're broadside, quartering, overhead, going away, or incoming shots.

Among those who know sea-duck hunting, almost everyone agrees that it's advisable for a gunning party to be armed with three or four boxes of shells per man. A hundred rounds per gun seems like an inordinate quantity of ammo in order to get a limit of seven ducks. If you're a super scattergunner and you don't take any long shots, you can probably get by with one box. That is, if someone else does the shooting on crippled birds.

Chasing cripples is where at least half of the shells are burned up on a sea-duck shoot. The back section of a sitting sea duck is the toughest part of his anatomy to penetrate. Also, it's highly likely that, just when you're pulling your trigger on him, he'll pop under the surface. Some innovative sea-duckers take along a box or two of BBs or T-shot in their arsenals, to be used on cripples. While there are fewer pellets in those loads, the pellets are bigger and have more punch. And, since it's not necessary to aim a few lengths ahead of a duck on the water, you can try for a head shot.

Recovering cripples may be a nuisance, because you have to up-anchor and track them down. But, as a sportsman, you're honor bound to follow up on them and avoid a waste of waterfowl.

As for your sea-duck arsenal, use the biggest weapon you can handle. Unless it's absolutely necessary, there's not much point in going smaller than a 12-gauge. Even slight shooters, with some practice, can handle a 12-gauge gun. The mighty 10-gauge used to be a rarity, but is finding increasing favor among goose hunters and sea-duckers.

Regardless of what type of firearm a sea-ducker uses, he should run pattern tests at different ranges and with different loads, and, if possible, with different chokes. This chapter is not supposed to be a profound treatise on shotgun ballistics, so I'll not go into the procedure for patterning your gun. But by all means, do some pattern testing; you may be surprised.

A hand-carved oldsquaw drake decoy, in contrast to a stuffed specimen.

Gunning for Sea Ducks

I have long held the belief that the ability of the *average* American hunter—whether he uses a shotgun, rifle, bow, handgun, slingshot, or whatever—to estimate shooting distances is about on a par with the ability of a McDonald's burger-slinger to execute an acceptable serving of Beef Wellington. Over the years, my belief has changed to a firm conviction that the average hunter is a lousy judge of shooting distances. Again, I emphasize the word "average."

I first became aware of this when I was practice-shooting with a guy who is a nationally acclaimed bowhunter. We were polishing our shooting the day before a special bowhunt for Sika deer at the Chincoteague National Wildlife Refuge on Virginia's Eastern Shore. We had set up a paper deer target on the ocean-fronted dunes where we anticipated we'd be flipping our arrows at Sikas the following day.

With the breaking Atlantic surf at our backs, I asked, "How far do you think we are from the target?"

"About 45 yards," he said. "What do you figure the range to be?"

I looked over the sandy terrain between us and the target, did some instant mental calculations, and said, with supreme confidence, "That range is not an inch over 30 yards. Let's step it off and see." We paced off the distance, which proved to be 31 yards. So I was off a few inches, but I was a helluva lot closer than his guess of 45 yards.

This is not a bragging session. I must explain that my ability to estimate yardage goes back to my prep school and college days, when I was a lacrosse goalie. The 100-yard lacrosse field is divided by a white 50-yard stripe. When my team had the ball on the attack at the other end of the field, the butterflies in my belly would relax. But when our opponents regained the ball, crossed that 50-yard marker, and came racing downfield at me, intent on bombarding me with a heavy rubber ball propelled at over 100 miles per

hour, my adrenaline flowed in on a high tide. That's why
the distance of 50 yards is imprinted forever in my mind.
For judging distances, it was a help too that I played foot-
ball. I can look at a piece of turf and visualize what five and
ten yards look like, because those are the yardages that
often represent the difference between a win or a loss.

No one is infallible, of course, especially me. I got my
comeuppance in Texas, where I was hunting Corsican rams
with Murry and Winston Burnham, makers of the famous
game calls. Murry was recounting a missed shot he had
taken that morning at a ram. "He was about 65 yards,"
Murry said, "about as far as that cottonwood tree over
yonder."

I said, "Murry, no wonder you missed; that cottonwood is at least 85 yards." To settle the argument, we
stepped off the distance to the cottonwood. It was 68 paces.
I felt like crawling into the nearest cactus patch and hiding
my head in shame. It must have been the purity of that Texas
air that threw me off.

All that probably has as much to do with estimating
waterfowl range as the Texas panhandle has to do with the
Great Lakes. When you're judging the distance from your
shotgun to a speeding sea duck, there's no intervening terra
firma to give you a clue to the range. If the bird is well above
the water, there's nothing between you and your target but
air. And if the duck is skimming the surface, you can't look
across the waves and get an accurate handle on the distance, because most everyone knows that distances over
water are deceptive.

When you hear a shotgunner say he dropped a duck
60 yards away, you can take that with a handful of sodium
chloride. Not that it can't happen; the point is: How does
he know it was 60 yards?

Recently, I brought up that point to a veteran sea-duck
gunner. He said, "It's simple. You place your farthest decoy

45 yards out. If a flight of sea ducks flies beyond that, you know you shouldn't shoot."

That's when I threw a zinger at him. "That's great," I said, "but, given the fact that it's tough to determine yardages accurately over water, how can you be sure that your estimate of 45 yards is on the beam, unless, of course, you take the trouble to use a range finder?"

Figuring the hunter-to-bird range is only one of the vital elements in duck shooting. To make a scoring shot, you must consider not only the distance but also the bird's speed, the angle of its flight, and the direction and force of the wind. In addition, you must know your weapon's capability, that is, the maximum effective distance combined with your gun's shot pattern at various yardages and with different loads.

In my own case, I try to pass up a shot if the bird is more distant than 45 yards. That's taking into consideration my known shooting capability with the gun and the loads I use. It's a personal, self-imposed limit and I'm certainly not suggesting it should apply to all gunners. If you're a terrific shot and you use a hard-hitting, full-choke gun, maybe a 10-gauge, that's nourished with maximum-load, three-inch magnums, and you've had years of experience with that combination, go ahead and take longer shots. But if you cripple very many birds that way, your popularity among the other gunners will drop precipitately.

There is a way to get a fairly good idea of how far away a flying duck is. I don't claim that it's an original discovery of mine, but I've never heard of anyone else who uses it. It's both simple and, once you think about it, obvious.

Using a yardstick, measure your normal stride. Let's say it's 30 inches. On an open, level lawn, place on the ground some kind of marker—a handkerchief, a stone, or your yardstick. Starting at your marker, step off 54 paces and put down another marker. Then calculate the yardage.

Use a yardstick to measure your stride.

If your normal stride is 30 inches and you walk 54 paces, you don't need a calculator to tell you that the distance is 45 yards.

Have someone stand at the second marker, holding at arm's length a duck decoy, preferably a sea-duck decoy or a mounted sea duck. Standing at the first marker with your shotgun—*make sure it's unloaded*—point the gun at the decoy, holding the bead of your front shotgun sight directly on the decoy. Take a mental photograph of how much area of the bogus duck is covered by your front-sight bead. Shoot that mental photo until your eye remembers the size of the bead in relation to the duck.

Then you'll have a fairly good idea about how to size up a duck at 45 yards. The same principle applies to goose shooting. Stride off your 54 paces, each of which measures 30 inches. Have someone hold up a full-size goose decoy or a freshly killed, fully feathered Canada goose. Align your front-sight bead on the body of the goose and note how much of the big bird's body is covered by that sight bead. Imprint the mental photograph on your memory.

This system is not as simple as it may seem, but with some practice and experience on birds, you'll find it's a big help in taking the guesswork out of estimating the range of waterfowl.

Once you've made an instant calculation of the range, however, you still have to consider those other factors—the angle of the bird's flight, its speed, and the direction and force of the wind. And, usually, before pulling the trigger, you'll have only a second or less to program all those factors into your brain's computer and get an instant mental printout.

The safety angle cannot be overemphasized in sea-duck shooting. Actually, that applies to any form of gunning, but is especially important in most types of sea-duck shoots. The best example occurs when you're in a boat with

Have someone hold up a sea duck and align it with your front-sight bead.

two or three other hunters and perhaps a guide. It's not like the situation in a blind where you and your companions are side by side in the same line and you usually have a 180-degree shooting angle. On a typical sea-duck shoot, you have a 360-degree scope. Don't get so excited that you swing on a low-flyer that's in line with one of your buddies. Work out your own plan of attack, such as designating gunners on the starboard side not to take shots at ducks coming in low on the left, and vice versa.

Keep your gun on safe at all times. If you don't already know how to do it, drill yourself in sliding off the safety when you're raising the gun for a shot. That should be a conditioned reflex, so you don't even have to think about it in the excitement of getting off a shot. Practice mounting your gun quickly and smoothly. That may seem elementary. You may be able to get that gun up neatly while on a shirt-sleeved dove shoot, but mounting your gun in a hurry is a lot different when you're wearing a bulky, down-filled hunting coat. Hold your shotgun in a comfortable, safe position, but be prepared to shoulder it at any time, because sea ducks often appear from out of nowhere.

7

What to Do with Your Sea Ducks

AN IMPORTANT purpose of this book, as was pointed out in Chapter 2, is to disabuse waterfowl hunters of the fatuous notion that sea ducks are not suitable table fare.

I'm convinced that the sea duck's reputation of being unfit for human consumption is the result of preparing a sea duck as you would any other duck—in other words, plucking it and then roasting the whole bird. I know this from firsthand experience, because the first sea duck I ever shot—that previously mentioned oldsquaw in 1947—was prepared in the usual way. It was a dismal, distasteful, culinary disaster.

I've asked a number of gunners who reject the idea of eating these birds if they've ever tried a sea-duck dinner. Without exception, the answer to my question is about the same: "No, I've never eaten those fishy ducks. Everyone says they're not worth the fuel to cook them."

"But, do you know personally anyone who has cooked and eaten sea ducks and didn't like them?" I ask, trying to pin him down.

"No, not really. But it's common knowledge that they're not fit to eat."

Gunning for Sea Ducks

Tell that to a veteran sea-ducker, and he may say, "Good. You just keep thinking that way, and if you get any sea ducks, give them to me. I'll take all I can get."

To use a culinary phrase, what it boils down to is how the fowl, sea duck or other, is prepared and cooked. A grain-fed mallard, if not properly handled in the kitchen, can bend your fork and taste like a roast of well-aged hunting boot.

When it comes to cooking the better-known duck species, there are dissenting schools of thought. Some hunters insist that their ducks be roasted so briefly that they're blood-running rare, so undercooked that you can almost hear them quack. At the opposite end of the dinner table are those who want a duck cooked until it's bone-dry, in which case the meat loses much of its distinctive flavor.

There's disagreement, too, as to how a duck should be handled before it reaches the kitchen. There are those duck hunters who believe the entrails should be removed promptly, even before leaving the blind, and some who think the birds' flavor is not affected if the ducks are not drawn until later in the evening of the hunt. Then there are some traditionalists who hang their drawn ducks for a few days before removing the feathers; this procedure is generally followed in Europe, where it is considered that all game birds should be hung for an extended period. When wild ducks were plentiful, up until 60 years ago, it was customary simply to remove the breasts, thus dispensing with the tedious problem of defeathering the birds, and at the same time discarding the less desirable parts of the carcass.

With sea ducks, my experience indicates that, while transporting the bag from the hunting area to the home, the birds should be spread apart so that they're not touching one another, thus dissipating their body heat as soon as possible. Upon reaching home, I don't bother with drawing the ducks, nor do I go through the laborious pluck-

108

ing process. Instead, using a sharp knife, I fillet out the breasts.

With your fingers, spread apart the feathers all along the breastbone; then, make an incision on either side of the breastbone, and slice downward to one side of it with the knife, keeping the blade tight against the bone, so as not to lose any of the meat. At the same time, peel the skin away from the meat, until the bare breast meat is fully exposed. After another cut with the knife, lift the fillet out. Repeat this process on the other side. It's important at this point to trim off every bit of fat, however small, from the duck breasts. That point cannot be overemphasized. Even tiny specks of fat will have an unsavory effect on the finished cooked product. From here on, follow any one of the following recipes.

A few hunting friends of mine merely flour the sea-duck breasts and cook them as they would fried chicken. I've tried this method, with such mixed results that I don't recommend it, although the few times it was successful, the breasts were as good as any other ducks I've eaten.

I've been told by an Eastern Shore hunting guide about a recipe for preparing sea ducks that made them taste no different from other wild ducks. It seems that about two decades ago, there was an elderly black woman who gave the initial treatment to a mixed bag of ducks—mallards, redheads, pintails, baldpates, black ducks, and sea ducks— whatever the gunners in the guide's family were able to shoot during the week. She scalded all the ducks, plucked them, then returned them to the guide's family, who had a duck dinner every Sunday during the season. The birds were refrigerated until Saturday, when they were all placed in a large tub filled with salted water. On Sunday, the family cook roasted all the ducks together, and, according to my guide friend, all the birds, including the sea ducks, tasted the same, which is to say—good.

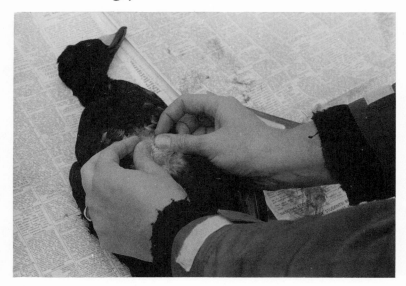

To start to fillet the breast meat from a sea duck, spread the
feathers apart along the breastbone.

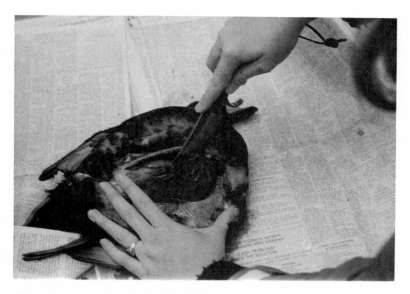

Slice downward with the knife, keeping the blade against the breastbone.

Peel the skin away from the meat, until the breast meat is fully exposed.

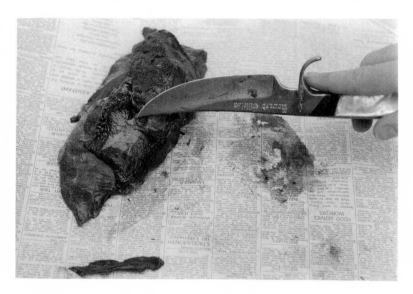

It's important to slice off every tiny bit of fat from the duck breast.

Gunning for Sea Ducks

A pair of filleted sea-duck breasts

What to Do with Your Sea Ducks

When I first became seriously interested in sea-ducking, back in 1970, I lived on a waterfront property that was improved by an old church, possibly nineteenth-century, that, complete with altar and choir loft, had been converted to a dwelling. Nobody knows whence the church got its name, but the more elderly native folk knew it as "Frogeye." It was there that I concocted the perfect sauce for any kind of waterfowl. It's called, quite properly, Frogeye Sauce, and it's good on the birds and on the accompanying wild rice. Here's the recipe, tried and true.

Grate the skin of two oranges, simmer lightly with about five ounces of sherry, then stir in three tablespoons of prepared mustard. When thoroughly blended, add one cup of currant jelly. Serve at once, or let it cool, then put it in a glass jar and store in your refrigerator (more on sauces later).

It was also during that time that a tasty sea-duck recipe evolved in the kitchen at Frogeye.

Soak sea-duck breasts overnight in a strong saltwater solution, with one-half cup of vinegar and one sliced onion. Before cooking, dry meat, rub with salt and pepper, and dredge with flour. Put a half-stick of butter or margarine in a heavy cast-iron skillet. Heat until butter is smoking, and put in meat. Brown both sides quickly, reduce flame, and cook slowly, covered. When the meat is tender, remove it to a warming oven. Add six ounces of sherry to skillet, then stir in four tablespoons of Frogeye Sauce. Blend thoroughly, pour over meat, and serve. The breasts should be sliced on the plates as thin as possible with a sharp knife. Believe it or not, the meat has something of the flavor of venison.

My friend, Porter Hopkins, who guns for sea ducks off the coast of Maine as well as on the Chesapeake Bay, says he eats all types of sea ducks, but he prefers eiders. He marinates the breast fillets overnight in a mixture of olive oil, vinegar, and lemon-and-pepper seasoning. Zesty Italian dressing makes a good marinade, too, he says. For good hors d'oeuvres that are different, Porter slices the meat thin and charcoal-broils it.

In Delaware, Bill Wise lets his wife do the cooking of his and his sons' sea ducks. She uses beef bouillon and cooks the breasts like Swiss steak.

In New England, scoters—or coots, as they're called there—are cooked in various ways. One method calls for frying a rasher of bacon (five or six slices) in a heavy cast-iron skillet over medium heat. When the bacon reaches the pre-crisp stage, remove it and put the sea-duck breasts in the sizzling bacon grease. Cover and cook for five minutes. Turn the breasts, cover them with bacon, and fry covered for about four minutes. Remove the breasts and the bacon to a warming oven. Add to the skillet about five ounces of red currant jelly. Stir until the jelly is melted. Serve the ducks and bacon, using the contents of the skillet as a sauce.

A highly recommended scoter treatment from the same area is like a stew and calls for marinating the breasts for 12 hours in a mixture of one-quarter cup of cider vinegar, a couple of thinly sliced onions, four whole cloves, two bay leaves, three cloves of garlic, minced, and salt and pepper. In a casserole or stewpot, fry four ounces of salt pork and, after draining and patting dry the duck breasts, brown them on both sides in the pork fat. Pour off the fat, put the salt pork pieces back into the pot and add the marinade, plus one chopped tomato and a half-teaspoon of dried tarragon. Add salt and pepper to taste. Cover the pot and cook for two hours at a low simmer.

Another New England sea-duck recipe involves putting six or eight breasts in a bowl and covering them with buttermilk. After they've been in the refrigerator two days, remove the meat and wipe it dry, saving the buttermilk. Meanwhile,

What to Do with Your Sea Ducks

fry a half-pound of bacon in a cast-iron skillet until crisp. Remove the bacon and sauté two cloves of crushed garlic in the bacon grease over medium heat. Remove the garlic before it browns and add to the skillet one chopped onion, two stalks of celery, finely sliced, and a half-teaspoon of basil. When the onions become soft, put in the duck breasts and brown them quickly. Add one-half cup of red wine and cook over medium heat for 20 minutes. Remove the solid ingredients with a slotted spoon and discard; add the reserved buttermilk, which can be reduced slightly to make a sauce. Serve the duck with the crisp bacon.

Ed Mikula, assistant chief of wildlife in Michigan's Department of Natural Resources, cooks his sea ducks along with bluebills and other species. He believes that it's important to remove the ducks' entrails as soon as possible after killing. He fillets the breast meat and adds it to a mixture of tomato sauce, chopped onions, celery, salt and pepper, mushrooms, and one-half cup of Burgundy wine. Then the mixture is slow-cooked for four to five hours.

Mike McBride and his wife Diane—as the reader may remember from Chapter 4—operate a lodge in China Poot Bay, near Homer, Alaska. They cook and eat hundreds of sea ducks each year, both fresh and frozen. They love eating them, and most of their guests agree. Here, in Mike's words, is how he and Diane handle sea ducks.

> Before freezing or eating fresh, I let the birds soak in a
> pail of salt water, and change the water two or three
> times to get rid of excess blood. We breast the sea ducks
> and make sure to get all the yellow and orange fat off.
> While there is still useful meat on the carcass, we put the
> remains in our crab pots; it's excellent bait and recycles to
> provide still another meal.
> We freeze them in double baggies, with about as many
> as two scooped hands will hold. I add a cup of salt water,

so they are immersed and protected from freezer-burn. Always label each unit; airline baggage tags, with little elastic strings, work perfectly.

The only way I like them cooked is outdoors on an open fire. Oak and other hardwood would be nice, but we have none in Alaska. Alder, which we use for smoking our salmon, is good, but the spruce is our norm, and while it burns a bit too hot, you want them charred on the outside and bloody in the middle. You must be sure to serve them outdoors! Really, this is critical, I think, and so are low-light conditions. No one wants to eat meat which actually is bloody in the middle. Once you put it on a plate and take it indoors to combine with other foods, while still good, some of the magic is gone. The night air, the dark, the meat sizzling on a grill, the dog asleep, or attentive nearby—well, it's a world all its own. We all know that the best restaurants spend as much time and money on décor and service as they do on ingredients and preparation. So the sea-duck chef must also set the scene to steal the show. You must eat the sea-duck breasts right off the fire, hot as blazes, with some fresh garlic slowly simmered in butter, with spices such as herbes de Provence, and sliced on a wood cutting board as thin as you can slice them. This is as fine as it comes.

Those who like gamey meats will like my favorite. Homemade bread, thick-sliced, with lots of paper-thin slices of cold duck breast, a liberal spread of good imported mustard, some lettuce, or just as is—fabulous in a duck blind for lunch the next day.

Duck pâté is found in many upscale food specialty shops. If you have any leftover cooked sea-duck meat, you can make your own and avoid the fancy prices of commercial pâté. Check a good cookbook for the procedure.

What to Do with Your Sea Ducks

As to what to serve with your sea ducks, wild rice is practically a must. Mashed potatoes, either white or sweet, or buttered parsley potatoes go well with duck, and, of course, a tossed salad and a loaf of crusty French bread. Green beans, peas, and carrots are good, too, but don't use strong vegetables like cabbage, cauliflower, and turnips.

A few words of warning. Now that steel shot is mandatory for waterfowl shooting, we must exercise care in preparing and eating our sea ducks. It hasn't happened to me—yet—but I imagine that one's molars would get quite a jolt when chomping down on a steel pellet embedded in a sea-duck breast. When breasting your ducks, be on the lookout for steel shot. Ditto when slicing the meat before and after cooking.

A good sauce adds zip to the meal. I like it on the meat and on the vegetables as well. I've already described how to make Frogeye Sauce, but here are a few other options.

If you use a duck recipe that leaves you with some pan drippings, add some flour for thickening, then stir in some currant jelly and a splash of sherry.

Pan drippings also come in handy to make an orange-based waterfowl sauce. Make a roux with three tablespoons of butter or margarine and a like amount of flour. Add it to the pan drippings, and season with salt, pepper, and paprika. Put in the grated peel of an orange and the heated juice of two oranges. Stir in a healthy slug of sherry, and you'll have a fine sauce.

Cumberland Sauce is another palatable addition to serve with sea ducks, or any wild game. It's more complicated, but well worth the trouble if you're gourmet-minded. The ingredients are:

Gunning for Sea Ducks

    six ounces currant jelly
    three tablespoons dry mustard
    grated peel from one orange
    two tablespoons each of lemon juice, orange
        juice, and sugar
    three ounces of Madeira
    one-half teaspoon each of salt and powdered
        ginger
    two egg yolks

Melt the currant jelly in a saucepan and let it cool for a few minutes. Meanwhile, make a paste with the dry mustard and a bit of water. Add the mustard paste to the saucepan, along with all the other ingredients. Whip with a wire whisk and bring to a boil. Reduce the heat and simmer for ten minutes.

Wine, both in the cooking and as an accompaniment to the dinner, is almost imperative for the full enjoyment of your sea ducks. The type of wine to drink with sea ducks or any other waterfowl is beyond controversy. Serve any good, reasonably heavy, red wine. If you drive a Rolls Royce, then you'd probably accompany your sea duck with a Château Lafite Rothschild. On the other hand, plebeian though it sounds, you can't go too far wrong with Gallo's Hearty Burgundy. Either way, the wine should be served at room temperature, unless your house is quite warm, in which case it's a good idea to pop your bottle into the fridge about five minutes before serving.

There's no legislation on the books proscribing the drinking of white or pink wine with game. So, if you insist, drink your white wine. But make it a full-bodied one, like a white Burgundy. And don't chill it beyond recognition.

Bon appétit.

8

The Future of Sea Ducks and Sea-Duck Hunting

IN PREDICTING what lies ahead in the realm of sea-duck hunting, one point stands out as a sure thing: namely, that this type of waterfowling will become more popular. It's a great sport, and, as more people are introduced to it, it will attract a snowballing bunch of enthusiasts. Aside from the fact that sea-duck hunting is in itself a challenging and desirable gunning sport, there's a negative reason for the near guarantee of a growth in the sport—the decline in the populations of other duck species.

As more restrictive but necessary regulations are imposed on hunters who pursue the traditional duck species, some of them will give up waterfowling entirely, as many have already done. That's especially applicable to those gunners who can recall the good old days of liberal bag limits, before the man-made devastation of the ducks' breeding areas that made necessary the lower bag limits and shortened hunting seasons.

But not all waterfowlers will give up their sport; many of them will try sea ducks and realize what they've been missing all these years. In those parts of the country where there are sea ducks but the birds have been attracting few gunners—such as the Pacific Coast—it seems highly likely that more waterfowlers will go after sea ducks. When some

121

of them try it and see what fast shooting it involves, the word will get around and more folks will try sea-ducking. In those states where wide-ranging sea ducks have turned up for the first time fairly recently, you can expect more interest in these species, particularly among those who have become disheartened at the limited shooting offered for other ducks.

That more or less takes care of the future of sea-duck hunting, but what about the future of sea ducks themselves? The relevant factors are breeding success, the continued availability of their food supplies, disease, and hunting pressure.

That last one—hunting pressure—is the easiest to control. If aerial surveys and other research indicate a decline in sea-duck populations, the federal authorities can reduce the bag limits or cut back on the number of hunting days, or both. But the other factors affecting the number of oldsquaws, eiders, scoters, and harlequins may be beyond the capability of waterfowl management.

Take breeding success, for example. Although these birds are hardy and resourceful, unfavorable weather during the nesting period could result in fewer of them coming south for the winter. And, believe it or not, lemmings can affect nesting sea ducks. The reason is that lemmings are the main food of most of the predators that are potential raiders of sea-duck nests for eggs and ducklings. If the annual lemming migration is normal or above, sea-duck nests are relatively safe from their major foes—Arctic foxes, gulls, jaegers, ravens, eagles, gyrfalcons, and even polar bears.

While they don't occur often, outbreaks of fowl cholera have been observed in waterfowl in California and Texas. In 1970, a significant outbreak of the disease was reported in the waters of Maryland and Virginia. Between 5,000 and 10,000 birds died of the disease, most of them oldsquaws and whitewing scoters, as well as some buffleheads and greenwing teal. Scientists were not able to determine precisely how the cholera originated, nor do they know why only sea ducks were the majority of the victims.

As for the food supply of sea ducks, we've already learned from Chapter 3 that for the most part they feed on mollusks—mussels, clams, oysters, barnacles, scallops—small crabs, and shrimp, although they also eat aquatic insects, small fish, fish eggs, and aquatic vegetable matter. It's reasonable to believe, therefore, that if these forms of aquatic life remain stable in their present quantities, sea ducks' diet will be ample. However, there's always the possibility that some hitherto-unknown disease could hit the food staples that sea ducks exist on. For instance, the flourishing oyster industry in some states has been dealt a serious blow by the diseases MSX and Dermo, which scientists have been researching, so far without finding a method of prevention or a cure.

Another threat is the continuing impact of man-made changes affecting the environment of sea ducks. As scientists Stott and Olson have pointed out (Chapter 4), the supply of invertebrate foods in coastal areas is threatened by increased domestic and industrial pollution, oil spillage, heated water discharges, and other calamitous intrusions by Homo sapiens.

It's interesting to read *Waterfowl Tomorrow*, a handsome 770-page book published in 1964 by the Department of the Interior. The book is filled with learned discourses on ducks and geese, including the final chapter, by the then-director of the Bureau of Sport Fisheries and Wildlife, Daniel H. Janzen. He posed several questions about the future of waterfowl, such as whether hunters can expect more restrictions, whether future duck and goose hunting will be available only to a privileged few, and other questions that were of concern to sportsmen a quarter of a century ago.

Gunning for Sea Ducks

The interesting point is that there's no mention of sea-duck hunting. In fact, sea-duck species are mostly ignored in the book, which has only a couple of one-line passing mentions of common scoters, oldsquaws, and king eiders.

To sum up, the future of sea-duck hunting and sea ducks looks good. In saying that, I'm not—to use a couple of metaphors—sticking my neck out or going out on a limb, because it's a sure thing, barring, of course, unfavorable interventions by Nature or Man.

Index

Index